ALAN HEEKS, sixty-five, has reinv..... .umselt, nis work and his relationships. He has been a successful entrepreneur, and is now an expert on sustainable living, co-founder of the Men Beyond 50 Network and author of *The Natural Advantage*. After a twenty-six-year marriage and two kids, he enjoyed a second adolescence in his fifties, and has recently remarried. He runs Hazel Hill Wood, a seventy-acre conservation woodland centre which has inspired him and many other men. Alan is a member of two men's groups, has lived in a cohousing community for six years and has led many groups on men's issues, finding your life purpose – and knowing where your towel is.

Praise for Alan Heeks:

'This is a wise and inspiring book for anyone looking for a refreshing but realistic approach to their senior years. Well-researched and grounded in everyday realities, *Out of the Woods* will help readers with all the normal disturbing issues of seniority, ranging from money and status, through to fitness, sex and a new sense of personal purpose. Warmly recommended.'

William Bloom, author of *Feeling Safe:*
How to be Strong and Positive in a Changing World

'If you want to avoid becoming just another Grumpy Old Man, this book provides a great tonic. But reinventing yourself isn't easy, which is why the helping hand provided by Alan Heeks might prove very useful!'

Jonathon Porritt, co-founder of Forum for the Future

'Men do suffer. They get themselves into all sorts of negative downward spirals. Alan beautifully brings his caring for life and all its mysteries into this great survival pack of a book for over fifties men. Citing the gurus of the Age of Compassion – Joanna Macy, Robert Bly, Kubler Ross and Harville Hendrix – *Out of the Woods* weaves a super intelligent path through life, pain and reality and I'm pretty sure will be referred to for years to come.'

'As an elder who walks his talk, Alan Heeks stands out as a beam of integrity and wisdom. His writing is inspiring and fresh for this demographic.'

Malcolm Stern, co-presenter of Channel 4's *Made for Each Other*, author and leading UK psychotherapist

'Alan Heeks is a new, refreshing and dare I say 'youthful' voice in the ageing conversation. His valuable guide will help men and women make sense of the inevitable shifts and changes that older age brings. And what makes this book essential reading for those making the transition into life beyond fifty is that it not only guides you through the changes and challenges of the here and now, but also helps the reader to consciously create a new and exciting path for later life.'

Glen Poole, director of Helping Men, UK co-ordinator for International Men's Day

'Alan Heeks is an initiator and a trailblazer. He has established an organic farm and a woodland retreat centre with a beautiful wooden ark of a building. He has taken people into the desert to search for the meaning of life. Whatever journey he embarks upon, he opens it up to others. This book is no exception. Alan explores those shady years where middle age slowly becomes old age, with courage and humour.'

Annie Spencer, workshop leader

'Although the ageing process is universal, men and women experience some of its tasks and challenges differently. So this excellent new book by Alan Heeks – the first comprehensive guidebook of its kind to be written specifically for men – is a welcome and much-needed addition to the eldering/sage-ing genre.'

Marian Van Eyk McCain, author of *Elderwoman: Reap the Wisdom, Feel the Power, Embrace the Joy*

'A humorous and resourceful almanac of wisdom gained from Alan Heeks' life journey. He has generously revealed his experiences so that men over fifty can rebuild their lives and discover their purpose to fulfilment. Alan demonstrates that by coming to terms with emotional communication, men over fifty can make the impossible possible.'

Siri Nirankar Singh, yoga teacher

OUT OF THE WOODS

Alan Heeks

howtobooks

Constable & Robinson Ltd
55–56 Russell Square
London WC1B 4HP
www.constablerobinson.com

First published in the UK by How To Books,
an imprint of Constable & Robinson Ltd., 2013

A copy of the British Library Cataloguing in Publication
Data is available from the British Library

ISBN 978-1-8452-8512-8 (paperback)
ISBN 978-1-4721-1002-2 (ebook)

Printed and bound in the UK

1 3 5 7 9 10 8 6 4 2

ACKNOWLEDGEMENTS

This book, like my own journey, has grown from contacts with hundreds of men, ranging from soul-searching in men's groups to chats in pubs. Thank you all. And especially to the Winchester men's group, which I've been part of since 1992, and the Men Beyond 50 weekend groups.

The help from my two closest colleagues has been outstanding and invaluable. Max Mackay-James, my business partner in the Men Beyond 50 Network, wrote the health chapter of the book and has led the creation of the expanded website, helped by Julie Ryan and Katherine Hanson. My PA, Sarah Menaldino, has preserved my sanity by keying in the manuscript, keeping it in order and helping out in lots of ways. Giles Lewis, Nikki Read and the team at How to Books have been a delight to work with, as have Tony Mulliken and the team at Midas.

Several men and women have shared their expertise and advised me on specific sections of the book. They include Agatha Rodgers, Bob Dungay, Derek Chase, Giles Chitty, Jennie Rowden and Robert Osborn.

I've learned a lot about midlife manhood from the women in my life: special thanks to my new wife Linda, my daughters Ella and Fran, my mother Peggy and to female friends and ex-partners who have smoothed or knocked corners off me along the way.

Many men have played a role as elder and mentor for me: especially my spiritual mentor, Neil Douglas-Klotz, and others, including Nayyer Hussain, Alan Kellas, David Owen, Giles Chitty and Robert Osborn. I also want to acknowledge my connection with men I've fallen out with, or where the friendship has simply ended. I have learned from you too.

Hazel Hill Wood, the seventy-acre woodland retreat centre I run near Salisbury, has been a deep source of wisdom and healing for me and many other men, old and young. The other special places I want to appreciate are the Findhorn Foundation in Scotland and the wild green landscapes of West Dorset where I live.

CONTENTS

Chapter 1

Guides, maps and the midlife prime

Youth is the period in which a man can be hopeless. But the power of hoping through everything, the knowledge that the soul survives its adventures, that great inspiration comes to the middle-aged.

G. K. CHESTERTON

Many men find the years beyond fifty are the happiest time of their life, but also the most changeable and bewildering – sometimes all in the same day. Yet it's also true that many men of this age feel lost in the woods, isolated, depressed and can't find their way out. So why the difference? It's not luck or chance, it's about life skills and learning to reinvent yourself when things fall apart.

Many men in their twenties to forties focus on work, marriage and kids: this gives them a good sense of purpose and belong-ing. But somewhere between the mid-forties and sixties, these familiar structures either dissolve or change radically. Careers run out of steam, marriages get stuck or entangled by affairs and kids leave home. It's a fair generalisation that many men lack the skills and support network to handle these shipwrecks.

Men like guides and maps: they want a clear procedure to get from here to there. Tuning up a maturing man for peak performance is trickier than tuning up a car, but this book offers clear methods to understand and improve all the typical situations you'll encounter: relationships, work, health, family and more. The aim is simple: to help you enjoy your prime years to the hilt and reap all the potential this life stage offers. To do this, you may need to gain new skills and wisdom, and clear some old roadblocks.

When I was forty-nine, my twenty-six year marriage finally broke down. In June, after our younger daughter's A levels, we told our kids we were splitting up. In July, a month before my fiftieth birthday, I moved out of the family home into a small, damp, rundown cottage in the country. Without this heartbreaking shipwreck, I would never have had all the joy, growth and new adventures of my fifties and sixties.

Around the age of fifty-two I coined the phrase 'You're never too old to have a happy adolescence'. These were the years when I found the thrills and spills of blind dates, had sex in a car for the first time and heard my Sixties classics on a decent hi-fi. The great thing about being a teen-fifty is that you've got money, wheels, a pad and no parents to hassle you. And having a lousy first adolescence made me value every bit of the second one.

Mark Twain said, 'The best way to learn fast is make a lot of mistakes in a short space of time'. I've crammed a lot of mistakes *and* learning into the years beyond fifty, and it's on offer in this book. You may need to make your own mistakes, but this book could help you avoid some painful ones. You'll also be learning from hundreds of other men whose stories I've shared. I still screw up and there are still days of gloom, but I really believe the happiest, wisest time of your life can be *now*.

Whether it's fatty foods or manky sweaters, most men don't like change, and it's a researched fact that men often ignore major problems, for instance with their health or relationships. To improve things, you need to take a step, start a journey. There's no satnav that can tell you where to go, but this book is a guide to good choices.

Out of the Woods won't tell you the way forward, but it can help you to figure it out. There are chapters on the major aspects of men's lives in this period, and the gifts and problems they may be facing. These chapters offer you tools to help you define your position, clear the fog and find a good route forward: a plan of where you want to go and how to get there. At the end of each chapter, a resources section details websites, books and organisations that can help you further.

The questions and changes of midlife can come up any time from your forties into your seventies, but I've used age fifty as a shorthand. Many men are in denial about being middle-aged or older: throw out your prejudices and believe you're as young as you feel. This book is also written to help those close to maturing men: partners, friends, children, professional counsellors, health advisors and others.

MEN BEYOND FIFTY: SOME OF THE ISSUES

It's pretty certain that the maturing phase won't be life as usual for most men. In fact, if you were a car, you'd be trading yourself in by now. This is a time when many marriages rust apart or have to recreate themselves; when kids leave home; when careers reach sudden ends; when parents become frail; when health becomes a focus of attention, not something you take for granted; and when you have to check if you zipped your flies up. It's the 'old fart' danger zone!

Manhood is often defined by three roles: protector, provider and progenitor. In the years beyond fifty, these roles shrink and even vanish. This can mean that men's sense of identity, manhood and self-worth is dissolved. It's tough: male egos have a fragile basis at best and now even that's wrecked. There may be upsides in all this: the marriage or the job may no longer suit you, and now you're free to choose again. But even the changes you choose to make involve losing what's familiar, piloting yourself through a sense of shipwreck and making some new starts: see Chapter 2 for more on how to do this. When you're half-drowned, clinging to a mouldy spar, you may be tempted to sink forever, but there will be a new dawn ahead somewhere.

> **Defining roles? Mine's a cheese and pickle.**

Having watched many men in their maturing years, I see a basic choice in how they react. Some narrow down and cling to the familiar: habits, people, work, and so on. Destructive coping methods like drinking, anger and gaming get used more often. This can't work long-term because time will erode the familiar bits you cling to and the negative habits will damage your health. The alternative is to widen your horizons, experiment and reinvent yourself. Below you will find more on how to apply this approach. Sorry if this sounds a bit earnest but it can actually be a lot of fun.

A new kind of adventure

If I had to pick the one quality that would help men most in midlife, it would be a sense of adventure. Not the kind of teenage lads' adventure where you nearly kill yourself. This is about trying something new, being someone new and having the courage to explore the unknown, both in yourself and around you. The sense of adventure means letting go of history, getting off your own case and not blaming or judging yourself for what's past. You may feel depressed or angry because you screwed up on a marriage, a job, whatever. *These feelings won't help anyone: put them behind you.*

One reason I like the image of shipwrecks is that you can see them either as a fresh start or as a disaster. When you're washed up in rags on an unknown shore, you can simply leave your history in the ocean. You may have had years of believing you're a lousy partner, a boring geek or whatever myth kept you in your rut. It's not easy to change those habits, but it's possible: shipwrecks can help, and so can this book. Adventures beyond fifty can fulfil some of the dreams of your youth, and more.

I'm not denying the seriousness of the crises you may face, but with a sense of adventure, at least you can find the gift in the problem. This needs courage and requires staying positive in the face of permanent setbacks as well as short-term ones. Most men who have prostate cancer won't die of it, but many will lose forever the ability to get erections and make love in the usual way: I know couples who have faced this ship-wreck, treated it as an adventure and have brought more depth and fun into their relationship. You need courage to overcome despair and support your partner if their health declines or the menopause knocks them sideways. And if you lose your job or retire, it takes a sense of adventure to see how to replace the sense of worth, of being needed, which even a low-key job can provide.

It's easy to be scared at this time of life, to see the years ahead as mainly decline and loss. There will be losses, but the sense of adventure can help you make the most of all you have *now*, instead of fretting because it won't last forever. If you think about men of your age and older, you'll probably see that the most cheerful and likeable have more problems to cope with than some of the gloomy ones.

One of the keys to adventure is what Buddhists call 'non-attachment'. This means accepting that you can't control many vital aspects of your life. It also means facing and going through your fear of losing something or someone that matters a lot to you: you can find help with this in Chapter 2.

In midlife, many relationships face shipwreck or salvage. It's a high-risk time for affairs, which are an escape from facing deeper issues. Whether you're renewing a long-term partnership or starting over, your intimacy skills may need tuning up. All this and more is covered in Chapter 3. There's plenty of evidence that beyond fifty can be the best sexual years of your life, but it won't happen by chance. See more in Chapter 10.

Big changes in your family situation are likely beyond fifty. Your parents may be getting dependent or approaching death. Your kids are probably becoming adults by now and you have to reinvent your relationship with them. Old tensions with brothers or sisters may blow up as you move into the maturing years. All this is covered in Chapter 6.

Reinventing your life purpose

Maybe the idea of life purpose is a new one to you. Lots of men make choices about work and relationships in their twenties and thirties which are not very conscious. In midlife you can choose again, and hopefully better: surely all those years under your belt must have some benefit? Believing you can make good choices may go against past form, but with the benefit of this book, it could be possible!

A classic risk of the midlife years and beyond is a sense of pointlessness about your life, feeling that you're just a Boring Old Fart or Grumpy Old Man. It's an understandable reaction to the loss of identity and worth described earlier. This is where the sense of adventure is called for, so you don't collapse in the shipwreck, but dig deeper in yourself and take the initiative. It's *you* who must reinvent *your* life purpose: other people or random circumstances can't do it for you.

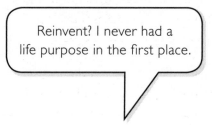

Reinvent? I never had a
life purpose in the first place.

If you ask a man in his twenties or thirties about his life purpose, he's likely to talk about success in work, making money and external achievements. But for maturing men, life purpose may be more subtle, inward, unspectacular. For example, it could be:

◆ Shifting your focus from the pain of past losses to enjoying all the goodies of the current moment.

◆ Deepening and widening who you are.

◆ Having a happy, quiet, single life after a marriage dissolves.

◆ Taking the role of an elder and helping others to fulfil themselves.

◆ Exploring interests and aspects of yourself which have been ignored until now.

◆ Fulfilling childhood dreams.

One landmark of midlife is coming to terms with death: realising that facing your dying can enrich your living. This is part of reinventing your life purpose in Chapter 8. Work is central to many men's sense of self, so Chapter 4 is also relevant: it covers work, money and fulfilment, including a process for re-visioning your work. Ideas like elderhood, legacy, bigger picture and giving back are all important in life purpose beyond fifty, and these are explored in Chapter 11.

Head, heart – and soul?

Many men rely on their brain and body to manage life. Handling emotions is not in the male curriculum, and a lot of addictive and angry behaviour by men arises because of this. The maturing phase needs men to expand the aspects of themselves which they are aware of and express. For many this means learning to be emotionally articulate: in other words, to say how you feel and hear how she feels, instead of blowing up. Less often, it means learning to use the talents of the brain and not be swamped by feelings.

What does it mean to be emotionally articulate? It really is like learning a new language – but one that men may resist because it takes them out of their control zone. The language of the heart includes a lot of sweet feelings such as joy, compassion and tenderness, as well as difficult ones. It takes time, skill and a safe setting for men to let themselves feel. This is harder than learning Italian! Part of the skill is in expressing emotions so they don't upset other people, by using methods like assertiveness, or Non-Violent Communication. See more in Chapter 3 Resources.

I *feel* angry. That's progress?

It's very different to hear 'I feel angry because your comment about my driving made me feel I'm not good enough' than 'You can stuff your putdowns about my driving, you bitch. *Your* driving is rubbish anyway and your cooking and...' There are many aspects to the emotional life. Part is how you handle your own feelings and process them. Part is how you express your emotions to others, hear theirs and face conflicts. This is important for intimate relationships and also for friendships, at work and in groups. You can find more on this in Chapter 3.

More controversial than the heart and emotions are the soul and spirit. For some men, these are meaningless, unprovable; for others, these are what give them a sense of purpose and stability. I am one of these men, and I'd simply urge you to give this consideration. Recall some of the most defining times in your life: the birth of a child, the death of a parent, inspiring music or landscapes, Princess Diana's funeral. I'd say that such experiences connect us with spirit – a dimension where all life is connected, where a higher wisdom or guidance can inspire us. You'll find more on this in Chapter 8.

How vintage is your body?

If your body was a car, what make, model and year would it be? Many men treat their body like a brand new Toyota 4x4 which can go anywhere and needs little maintenance. For men beyond fifty, the cars we remember from childhood are more relevant. The few Morris Minors, Austin Maestros, Ford Corsairs, Hillman Imps, Vauxhall Victors still on the road are vintage now: they need careful handling and frequent checks to escape the scrapheap.

As more of my friends reach the midlife years, I'm shocked that even men who have lived healthily can be hit by major illness, such as heart attacks or cancer. It doesn't help to walk in fear of such problems, but this is a time when good health doesn't happen by chance and when you need to be prepared if you do get ill. This means thinking about your support networks, both practical (eg medical professionals) and emotional: who would you turn to if you did need help? Chapter 5 looks at physical health issues, including fitness, diet and navigating serious illness.

Many people believe that body ailments reflect emotional or spiritual issues which have not been faced and cleared, and I share this view. Sorry if this sounds New Agey, but some of this is proven, like the physical damage from stress or depression. Try seeing illness as a message: your body wants to be healthy, so problems are telling you something. This matters even more for men, who may stuff feelings down for years and ignore body ailments because that's the alpha male way to do things. Chapter 7 explores emotional health, including depression, anger, facing addictions and alternative therapies.

Midlife crisis? Male menopause? Real or fantasy?

Are these concepts real or just a made-up basis for a juicy plot-line in Reggie Perrin, American Beauty, As Good as it Gets, and many more? It's true that the troubles of this time will feel like a crisis, shipwreck or even breakdown to many men. They face issues which undermine their sense of self and manhood, and which they're unprepared for. Men are often solitary, habitual and competitive, and struggle to handle emotions: now they need all the opposite qualities.

Terms like 'male menopause' suggest that there are predictable physical reasons for this crisis phase. Is this true? To some extent, yes: the drop in testosterone levels can lead to depression and more. The idea of male menopause may help people understand that this is a period of big change and upheaval for men, but it's not a predetermined set of symptoms. This book can show you how to prepare for these changes, how to handle them more easily and how to emerge in better shape than you went in. You don't have to make a drama out of a crisis!

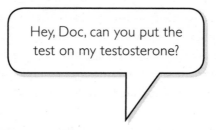

Hey, Doc, can you put the test on my testosterone?

Men and sheds

You may be wondering why men and sheds are so linked? Here's my take on this. I believe the image of the older man in his garden shed started out as a joke about the lousy social skills of older men and their lack of any private space in the home. They were imagined as furtively smoking their pipe, ogling girly magazines or whittling sticks. But then, in Australia, from the 1990s, a different kind of Men's Shed emerged: larger sheds where groups of men could meet to socialise and learn practical skills like woodturning or metalwork. There are now reportedly over 800 Men's Sheds in Australia, over 100 in Ireland and a growing number in the UK. They're a great way for older men to find new friends, new skills and more.

NEW BALLS PLEASE:
THE NEED FOR FRESH ROLE MODELS

Many male role models are thrusting alpha men in their twenties and thirties, which can make older men feel inferior. There are also plenty of midlife men who rely on naive masculine aggression: Simon Cowell, Alan Sugar, Jeremy Clarkson and many more – hardly useful role models for reinventing yourself.

In the maturing years it's really useful to lose your old sense of self and feel you're in the middle of nowhere without a map or compass. New role models can help you recreate yourself and find a sense of location again. It's worth spending some time exploring this, creating a map of possibilities. Here are some pointers you could use:

Character traits. Reflect on the qualities you would most like to have in this phase of your life and as you get older. What are the emotions you'd like to be feeling? Recognise that some of the characteristics you were striving for as a young man may be less relevant now and could be replaced. For example:

Alpha male	**Maturing man**
Controlling	Perceiving
Tough	Flexible
Achieving	Contented
Aggressive	Empathic
Narrow self	Expanded self
Excludes feminine	Integrates feminine

Men around you. Start observing men you know. Notice who seems at ease with themselves, which ones handle difficult changes well. What qualities do you see in them? Ask them how they sustain this. It could start a fruitful conversation.

Myth, film, fiction. These offer a rich source of role models. With characters you are drawn to, explore their qualities and see if these help you or not. Sometimes we are drawn to role models with similar struggles! The most useful characters may be more quiet and subtle. A role model who has touched me is Chauncey Gardener, played by Peter Sellers late in life, in the film *Being There*. Chauncey is like an innocent child in a maturing man's body, but his innocence touches hard-nosed players in the world of money and politics.

Archetypes. These are characters that can provide role models and help us connect with a strong resonance from others, real or fictional, who have embodied this archetype. Here are some examples of relevant ones for maturing men: *The Sage, The Good Father, The Peacemaker, The Hermit, The Wise King, The Deposed King* and *The Magical Child*. Perhaps the most important archetype for maturing men is *The Elder*, which deserves a separate section.

The Elder: A role model for maturity?

The Elder is a term you often find connected with maturing men, and I hear it in many men's groups. It's a word with various meanings, and maybe each man needs to search for its significance for him. This is a summary of what it means to me.

Traditional tribal cultures had a lot of wisdom still relevant to our times. Men beyond warrior age were elders. Although we imagine these tribes as hierarchies with a chief, many were guided and governed by the elders as a group. The elders carried the wisdom, knowledge and history of the tribe, and were respected for this. They guided, trained and initiated the young men. Elders resolved disputes, dreamed dreams, talked to the spirit world, wove stories and lived in a continuity between the present time, the past and ancestors, and the future – including their own death.

The role of the elder involves skills which many men in our times lack, but would be enriched by, such as collaborating with other mature men and supporting younger ones. See Chapter 11 for more on all this. However, we don't live in a tribal culture, or one that makes this easy and natural. This is one reason why men's groups are so vital, to encourage and recognise these traditional, archetypal roles.

SHIPWRECKS AND SUNRISE: ALAN'S STORY

Since I am your guide through this book, let me introduce myself by sharing some of my bumpy road towards maturity.

My parents were well-meaning but had poor parenting themselves. They were more demanding than supportive, more unsettling than steady. They expected me to behave like a responsible adult from an early age, so I built a facade and pretended. I was an only child till age twelve, always a loner at school and sometimes bullied. My social skills were poor – the talent I clung to was my quick mind. My teenage years were ghastly.

University, at Oxford in the Sixties, was the first time I began to find myself and enjoy being me. I started to feel my talents, my passion and glimmerings of self-worth, helped by finding good friends. While at Oxford I met Ruth, and we married in 1971. Overall it was a good marriage: we gave each other some of the steady parenting we lacked as kids and we had adventures we might never have had alone, like travelling through Africa and Afghanistan. The marriage helped each of us fulfil our individual paths – Ruth accepted my drive for a career and I supported her desire for children.

We had a happy time in our thirties, with two young daughters and my career flourishing. But the stresses that became shipwrecks in our forties were already there. I'd call our marriage a functional co-dependency: it worked well if we both stayed within limited roles, but by our forties we wanted to grow and change. I now realise that for much of my adult life I have been a workaholic. My addiction to my work produced impressive business results and good earnings, and it kept at bay my inner demons of low self-esteem, vulnerability, depression and more. But it limited my capacity for deeper happiness and intimacy.

> **He should be called Earnest, not Alan...**

My first major shipwreck was at age forty-two, in 1990. I did a week-long intensive course at Findhorn, a spiritual and personal development community in Scotland. Being among really open-hearted people, with a series of transforming processes, shipwrecked a lot of my rigid habits and defences. It started my journey to discover who I really am and want to be. And Findhorn also deepened my sense of spiritual connection. Since then, I've been seeking my higher purpose, the best way to serve the greater good. I've also been trying to lighten up and have more fun, but that's harder.

Also in 1990, I deliberately shipwrecked my management career. I quit my job as Managing Director, gave back the Jaguar and sat at home in my dining room reinventing myself as a consultant. I also founded an educational charity and led its work to create a 130-acre organic farm and education centre, The Magdalen Project in Dorset, which is still doing well more than twenty years later. This was an epic heroic struggle, very worthwhile, but it did little to change my workaholic habit.

I felt much freer in my forties than my thirties. I was no longer wearing suits, commuting, squeezed by business structures. I did a lot of therapy and personal development, which produced a variety of shipwrecks and sunrises. I trained as a workshop facilitator and led many groups, especially vision quests, and processes to help people, mostly men, fulfil their life purpose in their work. We teach what we need to learn! I was also exploring spiritual paths, especially Sufism, and going to stay at communities, ashrams and monasteries. Slowly, the urgency of my search grew less: I realised the journey is a wonderful adventure, and may never reach a final destination.

During the 1990s my marriage was under stress. The long-standing stability disappeared as I was in flux and Ruth was trying to find herself too. We both worked hard to reinvent the relationship, we went for couples counselling, but the hard truth was that we were growing apart. The prospect of the marriage ending terrified me, but it was a fear I had to face. This was the biggest, most complete shipwreck: in July 1998, just before my fiftieth birthday, I moved out of the family home in Winchester and into a rented cottage in a nearby village. I was living alone for the first time, I missed my daughters, I felt washed up, naked on an unknown shore.

The sense of lostness in my early fifties was deepened by my work commitments tapering off. I had time on my hands and I struggled with depression. The day-to-day sense was of being alone and off the map. Being single pushed me into new situations like soul mates ads and blind dates, which I felt entirely unprepared for. The repeated sense of being broken down forced me to find my essence, deepen my spiritual roots and reach out for new sources of support. The men's group I had co-founded in 1992 was one of these.

Out of this period of shipwreck new sunrises emerged. I slowly learned to enjoy living alone, finding pleasure in cooking and gardening for the first time. My second adolescence of dates and short-term relationships had a lot of delights as well as heartaches: my sense of myself was getting larger, lighter, happier. The various spiritual paths I had explored began to settle into a nourishing framework. Part of my work was creating a retreat centre at Hazel Hill, a seventy-acre wood near Salisbury, and my relationship with the wood became healing, inspiring and steadying. See more in Chapter 8.

In 2004 I gathered a small group of people and we started a small community and cohousing centre in Dorset – see Chapter 9 for more on this. Living in a community for five years was mostly delightful, often instructive and sometimes horrible. I saw sides of myself that I disliked, and changed some of them. It was another big chapter in reinventing myself.

At a dance group in 2006, I met Linda and we have been partners since soon after. In 2010 we left the cohousing community and bought a large old house near the Dorset coast in Bridport. We married in 2012. It's a very happy relationship, but also challenging. We are really honest with each other, the arguments are awful, but we sort out the problems and learn from them.

Deep connections with men have been a vital part of my life since my late forties. The deepest, most personally healing of all the workshop groups I've been part of are men's groups. There's a unique level of openness and transformation which men can attain with each other. I am part of two ongoing men's groups which provide this, as do the small number of deep friendships I have with men.

HOW TO USE THIS BOOK

It helps to be familiar with the detailed Contents on page vii. Maybe a crisis in one part of your life, such as divorce or redundancy, has prompted you to read this book: in which case you could start with the relevant chapter. However, many issues are connected and other chapters can help you with aspects of your situation. For example, if a crisis has left you feeling alone and bewildered, Chapters 8 and 9 are relevant on finding purpose and inspiration, and forming new friendships.

Reading the book from start to finish is another good way to use it! You could skip or skim chapters that don't seem relevant, but look out for resistance to a challenge: some parts that irritate you could be just what will help you most. Many chapters contain self-help exercises and all have a Resources section, which you can find at the end of each chapter. This book is not intended as a complete self-help manual, but it can show you where you need to go deeper, and methods to do so. It's similar to a general road atlas, which you'd supplement with a street atlas for a city, hiking maps for the mountains and hiring a guide if it's really challenging.

NOTES FOR WOMEN READERS

Men are much simpler mechanisms than women. Nothing changes them... Even when they have a midlife crisis, they do it in a mindless way... That's why I think we should let men go off and have affairs and drive fast cars and dream of being virile – and we should run the world.

GOLDIE HAWN

Unlike Goldie Hawn, all the women I've talked to about this book saw a need for it. If you are a woman reading this book, I'd like to welcome you and thank you for trying it. You may share my sense that some of the men who'd benefit from this book will be reluctant to read it and averse to change. I've tried to make it as engaging as possible for them. I decided that one way to help this was to address the whole book directly to men, even though there may be women reading it. There's a depth of safety that men find in all-male conversations, and occasional asides to women readers would detract from this. It means that you miss out on advice or resources which I could offer to the partners of maturing men, but hopefully you can now understand and support my reasoning.

Beware of showing off any knowledge of men which you have gained from reading the book. If reading this leads you to more understanding and compassion for your man, maybe give the book credit but don't let him feel that your knowledge is a threat to him. I know many women who have totally given up on men because they've been badly hurt and despair of finding a good one. Hopefully this book will show you how hard life can be for men, and encourage you to persist with us.

RESOURCES

All chapters in this book have detailed resources, offering more help and information on topics covered in the chapter. Since Chapter 1 is introductory, I have set out below my eleven best books for maturing men, which offer a variety of additional perspectives and help.

Getting the Love You Want: A Guide for Couples, by Harville Hendrix. ISBN 978-0743495929. There are dozens of books on relationships, and this is my favourite. It is based on decades of experience as a couples therapist and provides a wise, clear, very practical approach to evolving a wonderful partnership. He has also written a companion book for singles: Keeping the Love You Find.

Emotional Intelligence, by Daniel Goleman. ISBN 978-0747528302. This is written for men and women of any age, but it addresses one of the central problems for maturing men: how to become emotionally articulate in the inner life and with others. To live happily and working with emotional dynamics is far more important than mental IQ.

The Warmth of the Heart Prevents Your Body from Rusting, by Marie de Denezel. ISBN 978-1905744848. One of the best books I've found on ageing: especially useful for the young-old, who, as Marie observes, are often terrified of being old-old. This is a positive, practical guide to enjoying life at any age beyond fifty.

Aspects of the Masculine, by C. G. Jung. ISBN 978-0415307697. Carl Jung brilliantly blends psychology with the worlds of spirit, myth and everyday life. His original writings are very long, so this edited selection is a great way to get to his key ideas.

Desert Wisdom, by Neil Douglas Klotz. ISBN 978-1456516475. There are many ways into the spiritual realm, and this is a brilliant book for people of all ages and genders. There is immense diversity of insights, approaches and methods to explore, including the original truths of Christianity, Islam, Genesis, Sufism and other sources.

Iron John, by Robert Bly. ISBN 978-0712610704. Robert Bly is a leading figure in the US Men's Movement and a brilliant writer and poet. This book uses a folktale to explore the process of male initiation, including the role of the inner warrior and the elder.

The Rag and Bone Shop of the Heart: Poems for Men, edited by Robert Bly, James Hillman and Michael Meade. ISBN 978-0060924201. The editors are all leading figures in men's work, and this is a wide and wonderful collection, ranging across continents and centuries, with such section themes as Approach to Wildness, and The House of Fathers and Titans.

Home Coming: Reclaiming and Championing Your Inner Child, by John Bradshaw. ISBN 978-0749910549. This is a clear, compassionate guide to understanding the wounds of childhood, and an excellent self-help process for healing them.

The Last Barrier, by Reshad Feild. ISBN 978-1852301965. This is a moving account of a maturing man's progress through complete lostness to a Sufi path of illumination. It contains the immortal line: 'The purpose of the path is to bring a man to the point of bewilderment'.

New Passages, by Gail Sheehy. ISBN 978-0002556194. Subtitled *Predictable Crises of Adult Life*, this is a brilliant overview of the sequence of life stages which most people go through, with the differences for men and women, and insights on how to face them more easily.

The Tempest, by William Shakespeare. ISBN 978-1853262036. This was Shakespeare's last play. Its central character, Prospero, is believed to be semi-autobiographical and to express a lot of Shakespeare's own feelings about this life stage. The play starts with a physical shipwreck, an imagery that runs through the play, along with exploration of how to create a new life. A great play to read, and even better in live performance.

Chapter 2

Changes and renewal: The basic overhaul

Listen to this story: When the soul left the body, it was stopped by God at heaven's gates: 'You have returned just as you left! Life is a blessing of opportunity: where are the bumps and scratches left by the journey?'
POEM BY RUMI; TRANSLATION BY NEIL DOUGLAS-KLOTZ

When you renovate a house, you start with the foundations. There may be damp, rot or subsidence: you have to sort the groundwork out before you can build on it. The same applies to yourself: the overhaul has to start with some excavation and remedials, and that's what this chapter offers. It may feel like hard going at times, but it's a necessary prelude to the improvement works later in the book.

When I look back at myself in my forties, I cringe at how uptight and defensive I was. Working like crazy and getting stressed by all the challenges didn't make me happy. The break-up of my marriage destroyed my defences and habits: it forced me to look at the emotional baggage I'd carried for years. All the self-doubt, blaming others, fears and myths: I was way over the weight limit. Getting rid of the baggage has sometimes been painful – I'm still not rid of it all – but I'm far happier than I was before the shipwreck.

This chapter is a gentle guide through methods that have worked for me and other men. These include learning to grieve your losses, then celebrate and complete the letting-go. There's a useful road map of change, called the Hero's Journey. You can learn how to explore the different aspects or voices within you, to understand yourself better and how to create a support network to make these changes easier. And there's a section about home: choosing where you want to live. Finally you'll find a resources guide at the end of the chapter.

Most people have more change than they can handle, but the changes for men beyond fifty are extra hard: for many men, the sense of who you are and what you're worth is based on external measures, like what you do and what you earn. However, all this can change in a man's fifties and sixties. Often the shifts are imposed and a man has no say or control, which further corrodes his self-esteem. This is a period when redundancy is possible, when parents get fragile, when kids leave home, and sometimes partners too. Even if you choose to leave a career or a marriage, it's a deep shock to your identity. And health problems can be another blow to your self-worth and resilience. These are the kind of challenges I call shipwrecks.

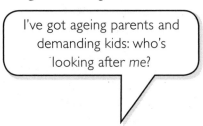

I've got ageing parents and demanding kids: who's looking after *me*?

Men often rate themselves against other men, and that can be painful in this phase of life. It's easy to look at men in their thirties and forties, enjoying fancier homes and cars than you've ever had, and to feel like you're yesterday's man. And some men in their fifties, sixties and older seem to be rampantly successful with their work, their younger partners and their health.

How does Salman Rushdie attract these beauties? Where does Clarkson get his energy from? Will Jeremy Paxman ever slow down? Before you get too sad at feeling old fartish, read on.

THE GIFT IN THE SHIPWRECK

Once or even several times in your maturing years, you may feel that your life is like a shipwreck – the ship of selfhood is pounded into pieces and you are washed up naked on an unknown shore. Well, good for you! To have a fulfilling life you need to reinvent yourself several times over. A few men can move into radical overhaul by choice, but many need a shipwreck every now and then.

How can these shipwrecks help us? They're the best chance to recognise and break some of the habits or repeating patterns which can run our lives. For example:

◆ *The Original Wound.* Many people create a series of experiences through their lives which repeat an original trauma. For example, a man whose mother left home when he was a kid may see his life as a succession of upsets where he is abandoned by a stream of women – especially partners, but maybe a boss, sister or friend. This pattern justifies the original wound – *my mother left me because all women do leave me.* There's familiar pain in this pattern, which some of us prefer to happiness!

◆ *Escape routes.* Men are rarely trained to handle their feelings or seek support. It's tempting to escape from painful emotions, conflicts and shipwrecks. The classic escape routes are addictions – alcohol, work, sex and many more – or doing something which distracts from the inner pain. A man who is prone to affairs, anger, violence and arguments with no substance is probably trying to escape. And depression is another kind of avoidance.

◆ *Worn-out toolkit.* Maybe your ship has to hit the rocks before you admit that the compass is buggered and the maps are out of date. Perhaps you got this far without showing your emotions, admitting you're lost or asking for help. Time for some new skills!

> **Ain't no drag, papa's got a brand new emotional toolbag...**

So the shipwrecks or crises can be seen as a wake-up call: a big enough shock to pull you out of your escape routes or repeating patterns. My observation of men aged forty-five to seventy is that this is a crucial period: either they face the underlying issues, reinvent themselves and flourish, or they carry on as before, in which case their health and happiness may well deteriorate.

Before you get too envious of mature men who still seem successful in classic male ways, ask yourself, have they really reinvented themselves or are they forcing themselves along in patterns which they can't sustain? And think of other men like this who suddenly failed, got ill and faded into obscurity. Major change may be hard, but the alternative is worse!

Try this exercise: Soul's journey

Read the lines by Rumi at the start of this chapter. Now imagine that you have a soul, a wise spiritual part of you, which has chosen all the circumstances of your life: your parents, partners, work and so on. You don't have to believe this forever, just try it for this exercise. Imagine that your soul chose these experiences to help it fulfil its purpose – which might be healing, learning, serving, or ...

Take some long, deep, relaxing breaths. Ask to make contact with your soul. Sit quietly for a few minutes, receptive to this link. If need be, ask again. When you feel a contact, ask your soul these questions:

◆ What is my soul's purpose in this life?

◆ What benefits would my soul like me to gain from my current difficulties?

◆ How can I do this?

◆ Where can I find help and support?

Take your time over this process, wait in silence for replies. Your soul may work at a slower speed than your worldly self. Conclude by thanking your soul for its help. Write down the answers you received.

HANDLING LOSS: HOW GRIEVING HELPS

Some of the biggest changes you face in your maturing years are likely to be losses. Major endings are really a form of bereavement: sometimes there's an actual death, like losing a parent, but many other changes are a kind of death in their impact on you. Ending a marriage or a job, kids leaving home, a bust-up with a close friend, moving house, parting from a team you've worked with — these are big transitions where the feelings of bereavement are likely and appropriate. This section offers you some pointers on how to handle major losses.

I told my ex-wife I'd miss her: isn't that enough?

The five stages of grief

Elizabeth Kubler Ross, a leading psychiatrist, suggested there is a cycle in the grief process, but also wisely observed that 'There is not a typical response to loss, as there is no typical loss'. Here's a summary of the five stages she identified:

1. Denial. This is when someone refuses to believe that news of a loss, or impending loss, is true. They carry on as usual. You may recall a friend who ignored a cancer diagnosis or insisted their wife had just left for a holiday.

2. Anger. It's easy for people hit by a loss to be overwhelmed with anger for a while: perhaps at themselves or the people directly involved, like a spouse who's leaving, or at society, the professionals who might have helped, or at God for letting this happen. Remember that anger often arises when someone is feeling vulnerable.

3. Bargaining. This stage is an attempt to make the problem go away, especially typical with a life-threatening illness, your own or someone close to you: 'If you take this away, then I will...' But this attempt to bargain and reverse the situation can also apply with relationships, redundancy and so on. It's rarely realistic, and realising it won't work often triggers the next stage.

4. Depression. A collapse of hope that the problem will go away. It involves accepting that you are human, prone to illness or death, and in a situation where you have virtually no influence over the event. Depression may be fuelled by guilt: a sense that this crisis could have been prevented if only you had done x, or hadn't done y. This calls for accepting yourself as you are, forgiving yourself and releasing the guilt. This letting go of hope is painful, but it's a prelude to facing reality and accepting it.

5. Acceptance. Once you accept that a painful event is happening and you can't prevent it, you have the chance to reinvent your sense of self and to seek a positive response.

Each of these stages can be quick or slow, and it's easy to get stuck along the line. I recently received an abusive letter from a man I'd had to fire over twenty years ago. I am sorry for his pain, sorry for the firing, but the one who has really suffered from his long-running anger is him. The stage where people most often get stuck is depression. See Resources at the end of this chapter and Chapter 7 for help in diagnosing and alleviating depression. One big way that grieving can help you is in moving through the depression phase.

Good grief

Yes, many men find it hard to feel and express their emotions. This is not silly: men are conditioned to be strong and protect the women and children around them. And men's sense of self is shaped by the opinions of other men, whose culture traditionally says, be tough.

Grief is the emotional suffering when someone or something that matters a lot to you disappears from your life. Grief is fitting *even if you ended it*. And the pain is about losing part of you, as well as something external. I recall a three-year relationship which my partner ended, out of the blue, in a single nightmarish phone call in which she listed the ways I was unfit to be her man. It took me months of grieving to get over this: not only did I miss the partner I loved and the relationship I was committed to, but also my self-image and self-esteem were truly shipwrecked, smashed to bits.

If you have a loss to grieve, how long should it take? Norms and comparisons don't help here. You may observe one friend taking two months to grieve a divorce, and another taking two years to get over a redundancy. What matters is that you grieve in your own way, at your own pace and thoroughly.

Did you ever see your father grieve? Most grieving for men is a private process, so you may have few role models. Learn what works for you. Solitude and privacy can be important, so you can fully let go into your feelings. Sitting in the pain of loss may seem hard, but it can be very healing. Finding the different voices within you (see page 30) can really help. It's quite typical to go back round the five stages above. And if you feel your grieving is taking a long time, accept it. So long as you're feeling the emotions fully, you're not stuck. Often the intensity of the present grief comes from the pain of an original wound (see page 22) which was never cleared. Now you have a chance to deal with the history.

At a men's weekend we got talking about losing fathers. Here's Paul's story:

My whole family are unemotional. At my dad's funeral, I was the only one who lost it and sobbed their heart out. It was my kids who comforted me, and we've been closer ever since. It was the sense of loss about growing up in a family where no one showed their love, that's what gutted me. But I definitely reckon I got through the bereavement quicker because I let my feelings out.

Does it help to share your grief with others? Maybe, but selectively. The people close to you may want you to be strong and unemotional, and can be upset if you're different. However, within a family it can help if you show feelings: many men feel sad that their father never showed his grief. In a safe setting, it can help a man's healing and self-esteem to share some of his pain. Doing this in a men's group is great if it's possible – or with a partner, friend or therapist. See this process like treating a physical wound: you have to clean the cut fully before it can heal.

Completion and celebration

A good way to finish the grieving process and to test if you're ready for this is to consider how you can complete and celebrate what you lost. With a partnership that's ended, it's a big mark of progress if the two of you can meet to give thanks for the good things you shared, appreciate the positives about each other, let go of the past phase and open a new one. When my father died, the closest family members had a weekend together, six months after his death, to scatter his ashes and share our memories. It was a lovely completion, which would have been impossible at the funeral, when the grieving had hardly begun.

Facing future fears

Our view of the future is commonly shaped by the past. If you've had difficult losses to cope with in the past, you may fear more in the future. This can really undermine your ability to enjoy the present and to make commitments for the years ahead. There are good processes to help with this in Susan Jeffers' book, *Feel the Fear and Do It Anyway* (see Resources). If worry about future losses is holding you back, her book offers ways to go fully into your fear and live with it.

INTO THE DARK WOOD AND OUT AGAIN: THE HERO'S JOURNEY

You may find talk of heroes and quests rather quaint in the twenty-first century, but there's a lot of wisdom in them. Joseph Campbell studied heroes and myths around the world, and he inspired American pioneers of men's development like Robert Bly.

Joseph Campbell used the term *The Hero's Journey* to describe the pattern of personal change found in myths all over the world – and used in many movies, such as *Star Wars*. I have simplified the original twelve stages to create a map of the change process which many men have found helpful, and which I've used with many groups.

1. *Leaving the Hearth.* You're unsettled in your daily life – you start to feel the call to adventure, but also a fear of the unknown. Somehow, you cross the threshold and make your start, you leave the familiar: this is already a brave commitment. You may not know what you're seeking or where to seek it, but you've started. Sometimes the Hero's Journey is both outer and inner: if you make a trek to the Himalayas or the Sahara, it can be a powerful spiritual journey as well as a physical one.

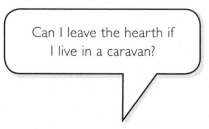

Can I leave the hearth if
I live in a caravan?

2. *The Early Journey.* Whether or not you have physically left home, you're on the road, exploring the new. You may recall this

stage in many myths and folk tales. There's the excitement of a fresh start, new experiences, and you're likely to meet guides and allies who give you insights, skills and tools to help you. You have uncoupled from the past and the habitual: you're already learning and changing.

3. *The Dark Wood.* Physically and symbolically, this is the stage of the journey where you feel lost, alone, in the dark, far from home. Where you know you can't control the situation and you don't have all the skills to get through. In this phase, the inner demons become huge, loud, tormenting. This can be fearsome, but the gift in the problem is that you can see your limitations, your fears, your demons clearly. I've taken this journey many times myself and led many men through it. The Dark Wood is the crucial stage in transformation.

This stage is the chance to let go of beliefs, habits and defences which no longer serve you. It's a time to feel painful emotions you normally push away, such as grief, and thus clear them. You should find that you can survive your nightmares, that your demons may torment you but won't destroy you, and if you really let go and open up, you find new strength in yourself and from other sources, such as friends, spiritual guides and contact with nature. In essence, this phase involves facing death, or your greatest fear, and coming through into something new.

I hoped the reward meant winning the lottery.

4. *Finding the Treasure.* This stage grows out of the one before. By facing your ordeal, you transform yourself and you earn the reward of the quest. This reward may be what you set out to seek, but it's often something different: maybe a new insight or skill. This stage may not be straightforward: you may face further

tests to earn the reward, you may struggle to understand what it is or lose it through carelessness. It's all there in the myths!

5. *The Hero's Return.* This can be the hardest stage. You have to leave the magical world of adventure, come out of the woods and find how to fit your new self into the everyday. Maybe the fourth stage put you back in touch with a long-held 'impossible' dream, and it can be painful to explore it – there may be hard changes for you or others. And if you return from your quest feeling different, will this be welcomed by people around you?

FINDING YOUR INNER VOICES

Carl Jung, the great pioneer of psychology, observes that in early adulthood we select a few of the many voices within us to be our adult self. In middle life, we either open the door to those other, ignored voices or they break in through the window. Within each of us there are many aspects, voices and sub-personalities. The ability to hear more of these voices and integrate them into an expanded sense of self can help you grow through loss and change.

There are many processes which can help you access these voices: some list the voices you might look for, such as the Inner Judge, the Magical Child and so on. These can be useful, especially if this approach is new to you, but you can simply choose to start listening and create your own map. Some voices will be a kind of inner recording of people who have influenced you. If one of your parents was controlling and judgemental, you may find their exact words coming back from the Inner Judge.

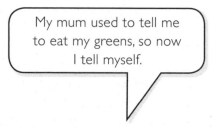

My mum used to tell me to eat my greens, so now I tell myself.

How can this help you? Often our inner air space is hogged by a few voices that keep grabbing the microphone, with a negative message. This is one way that unhelpful habits and patterns entrench themselves. For me, the Hurt Child alternating with the Inner Judge ('You're no good, you don't deserve any better, told you so' etc) was a powerful dismal combination, and it has taken hard work to get airtime for the positive voices. It doesn't help to suppress or ignore the negative voices: it's a matter of accepting them, helping them and not letting them run the show. The quieter voices can expand your sense of who you are, and give you confidence and fresh solutions.

I once had an amazing dream which I called Clapton and the Hermit. It showed me two major voices in me that seemed to conflict with each other. The Clapton voice wanted me to be famous and admired; the Hermit just wanted a quiet life in the woods. Then I had the stunning insight that I could be both: I could *alternate* between the limelight and solitude. Both voices could be heard and satisfied.

Try this exercise: Inner listening

In a quiet, safe space, get comfortable and take some long, relaxing breaths. Let your mind clear, let yourself be open and receptive. Invite any inner voices to speak to you. Welcome them, give them a hearing. After a few minutes, ask if there are other voices that want to speak. Invite your higher self to talk to you. Ask for advice on issues you are facing. Complete by thanking all these voices for their help.

Take a few minutes to digest your session: it may help to make some notes. If you repeat this process several times, it should deepen and you will receive a wider range of voices. You can ask the wiser voices to speak directly to aspects of yourself which are pained and confused. Sometimes you may find two voices in conflict: for example, one wanting to stay with a job or relationship, and the other wanting to leave. If so, ask other voices for their perspective and ask your higher self to arbitrate or give you an overview on how to proceed.

Voices in action: Martin's story

Martin grew up with a bullying father who always told him he wasn't good enough. His mother was a timid woman who never stood up for herself, or him. In Martin's mid-forties, his father died suddenly of a heart attack. When I met Martin ten years later, he had emerged from several years of depression, and voice dialogue with a counsellor's help had been the catalyst.

The first inner voice I found was the Fearful Child, and soon after, the Angry Father. I had taken in all my father's putdowns and they justified my low achievement in work, my failed marriage and lots more. Slowly I found the Higher Self, and a voice I call the Sweet Elder, which has echoes of older men who have given me support and good advice over the years.

Now I could start to converse with the Angry Father. I realised he was trying to protect me from further attacks and failures by keeping me on my toes. He was frightened, exhausted and needed my sympathy. Then, I began to hear the Magical Child, who had been squashed early on. It was healing and exciting to find a part of me that wanted to enjoy life, and could do so at my present age. Another voice which slowly emerged was the Good Mother: not my actual mother, but the way I wish she had been. Now I give myself some nurturing and I can accept it from my current girlfriend.

Working with a counsellor at first was invaluable for me. I wasn't used to this kind of thing, and in some sessions a lot of distress and anger came out that needed clearing. Now I can do the process for myself. If I get upset or have a problem to sort out, I make some time and convene a kind of internal meeting.

Who's in there? Surprises!

Discovering whole new aspects of yourself can be exciting and unsettling, like meeting family members you'd never heard of. This process takes time and courage: you may find that the old dominating voices resist, telling you this is rubbish. Try to negotiate with them, acknowledge their fears but ask them to support your wishes.

The hidden voices you find can be very different from your public personality: eccentric if you've been conventional, analytical if you've been creative, quiet if you've been exuberant, and vice versa. There may be some small, hurt pieces of you hiding fearfully since childhood that need comforting. You may also find a more feminine side in these voices. Many observers of maturing men see a shift to more feminine qualities as part of this life stage.

CREATING A SUPPORT NETWORK

The major change processes beyond fifty are demanding, both emotionally and physically. To handle them well needs support of various kinds, and even if you're not under much stress now, it makes sense to strengthen your support network. Here are some suggestions:

◆ *Close friends and buddies.* Find one or two people that can give you insights as well as sympathy when things get tough – ideally someone who has known you for several years, so they can challenge you on your patterns or habits. This could be a man or a woman: it should not be a partner.

> **'Thank you for your support: I'll always wear it.'**
> *Spike Milligan*

◆ *Professional help.* There are many benefits in some regular support from a counsellor, therapist or other professional – see Resources on page 38 for suggestions. The depth of insights, the way you can let go fully, the range of new skills and approaches you can learn: these are some of the ways a professional should support you in a way that a friend probably can't.

◆ *Spiritual practice.* If you have a spiritual path, it can be a deep source of strength and insights, especially in periods of major flux. For more on this, see Chapter 8.

◆ *Time in nature.* This could range from walks and rests in a favourite landscape to a longer retreat or vision quest. There is immense wisdom and nurturance to be found in nature: again, see Chapter 8.

◆ *Mentor/Elder.* I'm using these terms to mean someone who you feel has greater wisdom than you do, who cares about you and respects you, and could give you periodic insights and support: most likely a man, older than you, but maybe not. It could be a formal, ongoing arrangement, or ad hoc. This relationship can offer you a deeper perspective over longer time periods or for major issues.

◆ *Men's group.* You can get understanding, support and fun in a good men's group. And it can help you to feel that you're not a freak or a failure because you've got problems. See Chapter 9 for more.

◆ *Medical advisor.* Medical problems rarely give us advance notice, so it's worth setting up this kind of help even when you're healthy. Understand online resources, find a GP you can trust and someone you could turn to for a second opinion.

WHERE IS HOME? WHERE DO YOU WANT TO BE?

In the maturing years, there are many reasons why men may want to move home, or have to. Maybe your kids just left home and you can downsize to free up capital. Perhaps you're retiring or redundant and are finally free to leave the city. If your marriage is ending, you're probably facing a forced sale. Or maybe you just feel like a change. Whether your move is chosen or imposed, there's probably a loss you need to grieve – the end of an era.

This next move may have more freedom than you've ever had before: perhaps no work ties, no school catchments, no partner to agree with. Okay, it may have been forced on you and you may be almost broke, but look for the positives! Choosing a new home is a chance to shape who you become over the next few years and to create new possibilities. But this freedom of choice is something we rarely get and can find hard to handle. So here are some guidelines to help you:

- ◆ *Don't live out of a suitcase.* Being homeless is pretty stressful, especially if you're emotionally bruised from recent endings. Get yourself a temporary base, even if it's just a friend's spare room: it means you can have some belongings around you and a place to retreat and return to.

- ◆ *Envision your future, on all fronts.* Although one aspect of your life may be prompting the house move, like your work, consider your hopes on all fronts. Include work, social contacts, recreation, family links and partners – and needs, actual or potential.

- ◆ *Experiment for real.* If it's hard to decide between different ideas, don't just debate them in your head, try to experience them. A single friend of mine recently rented his flat out for six months and spent two months each in Totnes, London and living in a community.

- ◆ *Consider flexibility and fixity.* Be aware of how certain or not you feel about your preferences. This may be a good time to stay flexible: just rent somewhere or buy something that's easily saleable. But if you feel sure about your preferences for the longer term, indulge your eccentricities, buy the home you fancy and don't worry about resale!

- ◆ *Know your timeframe.* Are you thinking a home for the next six months, three years, fifteen years or beyond?

- ◆ *Test against future uncertainties.* Would your new choice of home and location work if you had health problems, if you found a new partner or if petrol cost £6 a litre?

RESOURCES

There are some good books, websites and organisations for this process, and it's worth investing time in this groundwork stage.

The gift in the shipwreck

Original wound: Facing and healing the original wound means understanding and clearing major issues from your childhood. This is sometimes called healing the inner child. Good resources for this include:

Homecoming: Reclaiming and Healing Your Inner Child, by John Bradshaw. ISBN 978-0749910549. An excellent, compassionate and powerful book with a series of processes you can guide yourself through: I have used it myself. John also offers CDs, DVDs and more on his website: www. johnbradshaw.com.

Hoffman Process: A powerful, intensive eight-day programme which can help clear major childhood issues. It has good credentials, capable and careful facilitators with a 1:8 ratio to students, and has been running for over forty years in the UK and elsewhere. I did the Process several years ago and found it very helpful. See: www.hoffmaninstitute.co.uk or call 01903 889990.

Escape routes/addiction (see Chapter 7 Resources)

Handling and expressing your feelings, and those of others, is important in an overhaul: see Chapter 3 Resources for more on this.

Who I am, by Pete Townshend. ISBN 978-0007466030. Pete's life story is an outstanding role model for facing huge, repeated shipwrecks and growing through them, but also for an example of the damage caused by unfaced childhood pain and the liberation of finally working through it.

Handling loss: How grieving helps

There are many good resources to help you understand and pass through the grieving process. Here are a few:

The five stages of grief: See a summary and more detail at www.facingbereavement.co.uk.

Grief: Symptoms and coping strategies: A good website, relevant to grief for many kinds of loss: www.helpguide.org/mental/grief_loss.htm.

Feel the Fear and Do It Anyway, by Susan Jeffers. ISBN 978-0091907075. Excellent for facing and clearing future fears.

Cruse Bereavement Care: One of the leading UK organisations helping bereaved people. The website has good advice and contact details for their many local branches. See: www.cruse-bereavementcare.org.uk.

Men and grief: There is some good material on how men feel and handle grief differently at www.menweb.org.

Moving on: The Hero's Journey

For a quick summary of Joseph Campbell's concept, see www.writersjourney.com, including the article by Christopher Vogler.

The Hero with a Thousand Faces, by Joseph Campbell. ISBN 978-1577315933. This is an inspiring book which gives the full story.

Finding your inner voices

There is a range of good processes and professional therapists who can help you with this, for example:

Embracing Our Selves: The Voice Dialogue Manual, by Hal Stone and Sidra Winkelman. ISBN 978-1882591060. Although published back in 1989, this is a classic in its category.

Voice Dialogue: There are books, workshops and individual therapists using this method. See: www.voicedialogue.org.uk.

Family Constellations: Don't be misled by the name. This is a powerful method to explore aspects of yourself and to clear relationship issues within your family, work team or friends, developed by German therapist, Bert Hellinger. There are many different websites for Constellations therapists. The only one I have personally used is Judith Hemming, see www.movingconstellations.com. Ask friends or do a web search on 'Family Constellations UK' and see who feels good for you.

Creating a support network

◆ Close friends and buddies: The amount of support you can receive and give could be increased by co-counselling: a training in the basics of counselling (eg hearing and clearing painful feelings), designed so that ordinary people can do it for each other. After the basic training, you can access local groups, weekend gatherings and other resources. There are two main organisations, each with a somewhat different approach. I prefer Co-Counselling International (www.co-counselling.org). The other, Re-evaluation Co-counselling (www.rc.org), has a more political edge.

◆ Professional help: This is a huge topic. You may want to ask your own contacts and do some web searching. Here are some brief pointers:

Counselling: Typically a less intensive, simpler approach than psychotherapy and may be easier as a first step for a few sessions. See: www.counselling-directory.org.uk.

Psychotherapy: Typically a more structured, longer-term approach, which can help deep-rooted issues. There are many different types of psychotherapy. One I like, which includes the spiritual dimension, is at www.ccpe.org.uk. For a much wider range and to find therapists specialising in men's issues, try www.bacp.co.uk.

Rebirthing: This is a therapy focused on breathwork and bodywork which I have found helpful over many years. See: www.rebirthingbreathwork.co.uk.

Chapter 3

A fresh look at relationships

Love at first sight is easy to understand; it's when two people have been looking at each other for a lifetime that it becomes a miracle.

AMY BLOOM

If this book was a travel guide, this chapter would be the Alps. The landscape of relationships can be both beautiful *and* deadly: you keep switching rapidly from heights to depths, paths are hard to follow – one false step can take you off a cliff – and the weather can change from sunshine to freezing fog in a moment. You don't venture up here without good guides and equipment.

If you don't fancy the mountains on your holiday, you can skip them, whereas relationships are central to a happy life, especially for men. This chapter is a guide to basic skills for this terrain, with pointers to the more intensive training and support you may need. As with the Alps, the feeling when you reach the top of the relationship mountain is wonderful. And in the maturing years, when kids and work are less big in your life and health worries may grow, a good partnership matters even more.

I feel well qualified to guide you in these mountains, having explored them intensely for years. This includes lots of peak experiences and most of the mistakes available. I've been lost, frostbitten, wiped out by avalanches, I've walked off precipices and slipped halfway down a cliff on small pebbles. I've had ecstasy and despair, sometimes on the same day, often with the same partner.

The major sections in this chapter are:

◆ Intimacy 101: Basic skills to help any relationship, new or old.

◆ Renewing a long-term partnership.

◆ The Danger Zone: Affairs.

◆ Handling a big break-up.

◆ Dating skills for maturing men.

◆ Relationship pitfalls: Co-dependency, flying boys and more.

Relationships can be tough at any age, but there are reasons why they get harder beyond fifty. Here are a few:

Divergence. If a couple have been together for some time, this life stage may bring you to divergent needs or values. When one partner gets keen on meditation and health food, while the other (male or female!) prefers boozing with the boys, something will have to give. At minimum, divergence means you both need to give each other more space and tolerance.

Affairs. The fifties and now sixties are a classic time for affairs, which can arise for a range of reasons for men, such as avoiding deeper intimacy with a long-term partner or an ego boost to offset failing potency in work or elsewhere. Affairs can be destructive, transforming, illuminating, fun or all of these together. See more in the section starting on page 51. They may arise from other pressures, like the next two.

Younger girl. There is an archetype of older men falling for younger women – sometimes leaving their same-age partner for good, sometimes having affairs. At an age when men's self-worth is getting hammered, it's very juicy to find a younger woman attracted to you. And it can offer escape from tough questions like how to renew an old, tired partnership.

Second adolescence. A lot of men had dull frustrating teenage years, so the chance to make up for this much later is seductive. There can be something quite healing about finally doing things you merely fantasised about before or saw in the movies, but it doesn't fit easily with a long-term relationship.

Health. A health crisis for either partner can transform a relationship, or kill it. A man may find great sweetness in caring for his partner – or not. A woman may walk away because nursing her man feels like sacrificing herself – or not. Health issues often force a couple to face questions they have ignored for years.

Existential angst. Somewhere beyond fifty, it's fitting for a man to question the purpose of his life, the universe and... everything. But if your partner is not in questioning mode and wants you how you've always been, you may need to be out of the relationship to find space to ponder.

Sometimes I don't know if it's angst or indigestion!

Dying parents. How men react to a parent dying varies hugely. It can be a catalyst for fierce questioning of everything about your current way of life – including your relationship. It can lead to depression or a wild sense of freedom. This kind of challenge can break over you both like a tsunami, even if your partner has supported you through the bereavement.

Kids growing up. In your thirties and forties, it's easy to lose the sparkle of your relationship in a focus on the family. As the kids finish school, need you less and leave home, you either need to reinvent the relationship or go your separate ways. My wife and I saw this need when our daughters were thirteen and fifteen. We spent several years trying to rebuild the marriage, but ultimately failed.

INTIMACY 101: THE BASICS

If a couple want a deeply loving, stable, resilient partnership, they need intimacy. Intimacy is a quality of loving connectedness, openness and trust between two people, where both are engaged in the relationship and there is a two-way flow between them. Intimacy can include the emotional, spiritual and physical levels: it can be found in deep friendships as well as your main partnership. You see plenty of couples who get by for years on something else – co-dependence, role-playing, interlocking addictions: but I challenge you to find a couple without intimacy who are deeply happy and resilient to the shocks life can bring. Intimacy is difficult and threatening for most men, for reasons we'll explore shortly.

If you can find the courage and skills to deepen intimacy, the pay-off is huge in your main partnership, as well as with friends and work colleagues. There's a basic reason why intimacy is hard for all couples, which is the type of partners we're attracted to. This is explained with beautiful clarity in my favourite book on relationships, by Harville Hendrix (see Resources). He has been a couples therapist for over thirty years, and his experience shows this: 'People are attracted to partners with the same characteristics (positive and negative) as their parents, with the subconscious hope that this partner will give them whatever good things the parents failed to give them'. Think about this and read his book – it explains how this arises, the implications and how to overcome them.

On top of this basic challenge, there are many reasons why intimacy is difficult and scary for most men. It threatens basic coping mechanisms and conditioning about what it means to be a man. Conditioning means beliefs that were imposed on you in childhood and become so hard-wired you take them for granted, such as being strong and not showing your feelings. Intimacy needs 'feminine' skills like intuition and empathy. Let's look further at common intimacy problems for men:

- Men have often been hurt and shamed for showing feelings in childhood and beyond.

- Most men are conditioned that they need to be strong and supportive of the main woman in their life (first their mother, then their partner).

- Generally speaking, men don't have much emotional intelligence, however bright they may be in other ways – ie, they are poor at expressing their own feelings to their partner and hearing hers. Men will do a lot to avoid such stressful situations, including resorting to addiction, anger, withdrawal and even violence.

- Men are often conditioned to feel responsible for the feelings of the woman closest to them: not only are any difficult feelings their fault (they caused them), but it's down to the man to make it right, and *make* the woman happy. This is *not true*!

- Men commonly believe that if they show feelings or vulnerability – what they'd call weakness – they will be pounced on and taken advantage of, as they may have been before. But it's a risk you have to take to deepen the relationship.

- Male perceptions of women are coloured by a mass of projections, fears and expectations. A projection means a belief about someone which you impose, which comes from your prejudices, not the reality of the other person. A woman can be a trophy, a saviour, a destroyer and more.

Try this exercise: Fears of intimacy

This two-part exercise will help you understand what your fears of intimacy are, and some of your ways of avoiding them.

1. Imagine yourself in a deeply intimate, ongoing relationship where you are completely open to your partner. Take a few minutes to imagine as deeply as possible how this feels, including its pleasures. Now see if any fear comes up, and explore in detail what you are afraid of. What could go wrong? How could this hurt you? Can you relate these fears to experiences in childhood or in earlier relationships?

2. If you are in a steady relationship now, do this exercise in the present. If not, go back to the most recent time when you were. Review your behaviour during a typical week of the relationship: identify the ways you and your partner avoided opportunities for intimacy. Intimacy here does not just mean physical, but also emotional and spiritual.

You can probably see by now how huge and difficult this topic is. If you feel your relationship needs deeper intimacy and you have a lot to learn, don't blame yourself or beat yourself up. Your partner may say she's desperate for intimacy and may blame you for the lack of it, but if you have a resistance to intimacy, it's pretty sure that she has one too, and that your avoidance of closeness has some pay-off for her. Don't judge yourself too hard and don't be impatient: this is a lifetime work.

For me, the term *fear of intimacy* is an understatement: terror is more accurate. I've been aware of my terror for twenty years, and have put a lot of care into healing it – on my own, with partners, with professional help. Over these years, I have made massive progress, but still have a long way to go.

This section, Intimacy 101, aims to give you both insights into the issues and a basic manual to steer you through this confusing terrain.

1. *Agree ground rules and honour them.* Sexual fidelity is often the crucial one – but ensure you know and agree about whatever matters deeply to both of you – it could be money, handling conflicts or who takes the rubbish out.

2. *Keep communicating honestly.* Have regular check-ins. Even if your habit is to keep your feelings to yourself, make a major effort to share with your partner what's really going on for you – but make sure you express emotions carefully (see box on pages 47–8).

3. *Know your fears and avoidance tricks around intimacy, and consciously try to change them.* You may have deep habits which look like unchangeable parts of your life (such as a demanding job or health problems), which enable you to reduce intimacy. Admit these to your partner, ask her to support you as you work to improve intimacy despite them.

4. *When you're upset, take responsibility.* Probably your partner did something which 'caused' your upset: but *your* reactions are *your* responsibility. Look at your own emotional patterns and see what old distress is aggravating your current reaction. Probably childhood feelings are running, so start by parenting yourself. Only when you are calmer, talk to your partner about what they did that upset you.

5. *If you're angry, don't suppress it and don't dump it.* Anger is one of the strongest and most dangerous emotions, whether it explodes onto other people or gets stuffed down inside, causing depression. Learn the methods of anger management, take a workshop, see a counsellor, and use these methods alone and with your partner.

6. *When it gets really bad, keep physical contact.* Sometimes feelings are so raw that words can only make things worse. Just holding each other or swapping some loving touch can help both of you feel connected and safer.

7. *Know what projections you put on each other and don't be run by them.* Most of us project onto our partner the difficult aspects of our opposite-sex parent in childhood. I had a controlling mother, so I see my partner's current actions through that lens. It really helps to know what you're projecting. Name it to your partner and check your emotions to filter this out, *before* you express feelings to her.

8. *Stay open, keep giving.* Your partner may be acting shabbily, dumping emotions and projections onto you or acting aloof. You may have good reasons to be angry, to shut down and to stop putting yourself into the relationship. I can recall going for weeks on end with my partner and me just sulking. Do all you can to keep your heart open, to keep giving your love even when you're hurting, to see her behaviour as coming from her pain, her patterns, not from malice. If you can stay open and keep giving, you will grow from the experience and you'll both reap the rewards.

9. *Treat relationships as a project.* This advice may appal women – but I'm writing mainly for men. Like other important projects, be clear where you want to get to, see what new skills you need and invest time to learn them. And get support – from close friends, from a men's group, from workshops or from a professional. This is a project of the heart, with huge pay-offs.

COMMUNICATION SKILLS: SOME BASICS

This is a very brief start on a vital topic, also known as assertiveness. For more help, see Resources on page 64.

◆ *Use 'I' statements.* Own your feelings instead of blaming. It's easier for the other person to hear 'I feel upset' than 'You're upsetting me'.

◆ *Stay in the present.* Talk about the present situation; don't generalise or add on past grievances.

- **Be specific.** For example, 'When you ignored my question, I felt upset' gives the other person clear information which helps them understand you.

- **Be constructive.** Ask for what you'd like from the other person, gently, not insistently.

- **Listen and seek understanding.** Ask the other person about their feelings and clarify what actually happened. Many conflicts arise from misunderstandings.

- **Be clear and direct.** Avoid sarcasm. And don't expect the other person to read your mind or pick up every hint you drop.

- **Don't escalate: calmly repeat.** If you feel the other person is not hearing a key statement or request from you, just repeat it calmly. And again if need be. Don't lose your temper or exaggerate to get through.

- **Acknowledge the other person.** It will help the other person if you assure them you hear their feelings and can see their point of view. This is not the same as agreeing with them!

REVIVING A LONG-TERM RELATIONSHIP

Marriage has no guarantees. If that's what you're looking for, go live with a car battery.

ERMA BOMBECK

My marriage lasted twenty-six years, but I still feel some envy at couples who are together after thirty- or forty-plus years. The joys of all that shared time, the richness of the family network, the many corners you knocked off each other: there's a lot to value in a really long-term relationship. I know several couples in their sixties, seventies and eighties with the sweetness of fully matured wine. And I also see couples who seem dead, bitter and grumpy. There's no one right answer: what is pretty certain is that your relationship will have to face the same process of shipwreck and reinvention as you do.

If things are sticky, you could use a method called *benchmarking* in the business world. This means finding and understanding examples of the good qualities you want. Through the long happy times of my marriage, we were friends with two couples who were about ten years older than us, and we learned a lot from their successes and problems. Doing relationship workshops with other couples is another way to gather more know-how.

Don't jump the red light

Basic advice if you realise your relationship is in trouble: *slow down, face it and explore the issues together.* This is often hard to do. Maybe your problems on other fronts feel overwhelming, maybe you doubt your skills to handle these, maybe you're high with love and adrenaline from a new amour, maybe you and your partner are already sulking in silence at opposite ends of the house. Whether you eventually stay together or split, your current partner deserves care and respect. Even if she is behaving outrageously, in hindsight you'll feel better if you do the right thing, which typically means a ceasefire, a period when both of you stop behaviour which could kill the relationship, and when you seek some outside help.

While it may be hard amid such intensity, a relationship crisis is a great time to deepen your self-understanding. You will certainly have masses of data and scope for major choices, so try to take some time out for reflection. Use the Inner Voices method from Chapter 2 to clarify what's really going on for you, which parts of you are driving your car. Even if your relationship is not in crisis, any long-term relationship needs some maintenance and overhaul. Look at the section below on pitfalls such as co-dependency to understand patterns you may need to change.

Deeper intimacy skills will almost certainly be crucial to achieve this: use the section above, and this chapter's Resources.

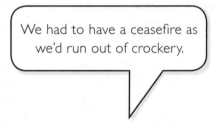

We had to have a ceasefire as we'd run out of crockery.

One of the commonest problems in renewing a long-term relationship is where one partner is ready for change and the other is resisting. Start with patience and gentle persuasion, but you may have to give an ultimatum. Ask for the changes you want, constructively and without blame, and set a deadline. Be patient if she starts to change but not as you expected. Suggest processes that could help you both, such as couples counselling, but be clear about your bottom line. It's actually fair to you and your partner to say, for example, that if she is unwilling to explore change over the next six months, you would consider separation and divorce.

Space in your togetherness

Let there be spaces in your togetherness.

KAHLIL GIBRAN, THE PROPHET

Renewing a long-term partnership will pretty surely mean both partners having space, more time and freedom as individuals, and scope to develop new interests and friendships separately from their partner. This is especially vital for men, who have often felt confined by obligations of work, family and bread-winning. You may need time alone and a chance for adventures. Your partner needs to gather enough self-confidence and trust to support this, and you need to honour the ground rules as you explore your freedom. Both of you will need intimacy skills to adjust to the other one changing.

Alongside more separation and freedom, renewing couples need to find a fresh togetherness: new activities they both enjoy, which can deepen the relationship. This could be a new sport, a creative hobby or volunteering together: giving something back to people who need it. The Harville Hendrix book listed in Resources includes an excellent ten-step process which is the best I know for helping couples to recover and deepen intimacy, and strengthen the love and understanding between them. This process typically takes ten weeks: some of the exercises are quite difficult, and it may be worth having professional support while you do it.

Mike and Lou are now in their mid-sixties, and have been married for over forty years. I've known them for nearly twenty years, and have admired their togetherness as a couple. I've also noticed that in recent years they seem less together, but still very happy. I asked Mike how it has worked for them.

Mike: *I got quite depressed several years ago when I was made redundant, and it did stress the relationship. I felt Lou was bossing me about, and we started arguing: we saw we'd got too close, our lives were too shared. Lou had to stop depending on me so much, and find her own strength. I had to stop worrying about her approval.*

I started doing things on my own and with men friends, and Lou amazed me by starting a small business. If we have a secret to success, it's tolerating each other, being civil and being friends.

THE DANGER ZONE: AFFAIRS

If you read the experts in books or websites, the basic advice is, **don't do it**. You'll find comments like *Over 80% of affairs end unhappily, Someone is bound to get hurt, It won't solve anything.* I strongly agree with these views. But I know that if you're a man having an affair, or on the brink of one, you'll find this advice almost impossible to accept. When you're on a high of testosterone and adrenaline, you'll look anywhere for advice that supports your desire. If you're in this situation, take a week of time out, go somewhere calm like a wood or a monastery, then read this section and some of the material in Resources. Also, try to find a friend who is truly unbiased, and review your situation and intentions with him.

Men like to imagine that affairs happen between guys with a long-term partner and an available single woman. In truth, a lot of women in committed relationships have affairs too. So maybe you're the one who feels betrayed and bewildered, and it's your partner who seems unreachable. This section will deal with both scenarios, but focusing more on men having affairs.

Men in affairs – Probing questions

If you're a man having an affair, or wanting to, use these questions to understand what's really going on and to clarify your course of action. Ask both an impartial friend and a professional counsellor to go through this process with you, since a large part of you won't want to find the real answers.

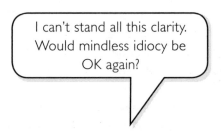

I can't stand all this clarity. Would mindless idiocy be OK again?

◆ What deeper, underlying needs are you trying to fulfil here? For example, escape from other problems, confidence boosting or revenge? Are there better ways to meet these needs?

◆ This situation is probably taking a lot of your attention. What issues are you avoiding or escaping? What do you need to do to face these appropriately?

◆ Who are you attacking by your behaviour? For example, your mother, a previous partner who hurt you, women in general? Are there wounds you need to heal and anger you need to clear?

◆ At a deep, maybe unconscious level, what outcome do you want to create in your main relationship? Do you want a reason to end it? Do you want to punish your partner for something? Do you want to prove you're not good enough?

◆ Explore what the other woman means to you: what qualities in yourself or your main partner are you trying to find? Celebrate these qualities in the other woman, but realise that you can find them elsewhere.

◆ In your heart, do you want your current relationship to continue or end? If you want it to continue, clarify what changes you want from your partner, what changes you are offering and how to start negotiations. If you want it to finish, explore how to do this as kindly as possible.

Whatever conclusions you reach, you will need other sections of this chapter, especially Intimacy 101, and some of the Resources on page 66, which include excellent advice, tools for understanding and support about affairs. In speaking to your current partner, communicate cleanly about your feelings and your needs. It may be tempting to blame and criticise her to justify yourself, but don't go there – it will leave lasting scars.

Ending an affair, or turning away from having one, may leave you feeling flat, bereft and depressed. It's a heroic thing to do, but few people will be able to recognise and appreciate your heroism, least of all your current partner. Make a real effort to find a couple of male friends who will understand and support you, and get professional help too.

Five types of affair

One of several useful websites in this field is www.affairs-help. com, which is based on the work of an American expert, Emily Brown. Her list of five types of affairs is useful, whether you are trying to understand your own or your partner's behaviour.

1. *Conflict Avoidance Affair.* When one or both partners are scared of conflict, where problems in the relationship can't be faced and needs are met through the affair.

2. *Intimacy Avoidance Affair.* When one or both partners are afraid of real intimacy, the emotional connection with each other can happen through frequent and intense conflict. Often, each partner becomes involved in an affair: it's a great reason for further disputes.

3. *Sexual Addiction Affair.* Sex addicts use sex over and over again to numb inner pain and emptiness, much like alcoholics use alcohol. Among married couples, men are sex addicts more often than women.

4. *Split Self Affair.* This arises when both partners have sacrificed their own feelings and needs to take care of others, and the deprivation has caught up with one or both of them. The inner split between self-fulfilment and caring for others is not faced and the affair provides an escape from facing it.

5. *Exit Affair.* One partner has already decided to leave the relationship and the affair provides the justification. The other partner usually blames the affair, rather than looking at how the relationship got to this point.

Your partner's affair – Probing questions

If your partner is having an affair, or close to having one, this can be harder to handle than if you are. Crucial decisions are not in your control: will she take time out, will she look deeply at her behaviour, will she even talk to you? Maybe you are too furious, shocked or untrusting to communicate well with her. If there's already uproar between you, try getting help from a couples counsellor just to start communicating with each other again.

Where possible, ask your partner to look at similar probing questions to those above, with an unbiased friend *and* professional help. If she does, you have the basis for a dialogue; if she doesn't, you may have to reach some unilateral decisions. Either way, here are some probing questions for *you* to consider, with help.

◆ What are your main feelings about your partner's behaviour? Have you felt these before? Does the current situation remind you of an earlier one and are old feelings inflaming present ones? If so, can you process the old feelings and separate them from the present?

◆ How is your partner's behaviour *serving* you? For example, does it confirm your belief pattern that women always let you down or that you're never good enough?

◆ Do *you* want this relationship to continue or end? If you want it to continue, what changes do you need from your partner, what changes are you offering and how could you move forward together?

◆ How have your behaviour and attitudes helped to cause the current situation? Are you willing to change them?

◆ Whether you continue or finish with your partner, how can you minimise the risk of you being further hurt or abused? Do you need to set ground rules, deadlines and conditions?

◆ Do you have enough support, as individuals and as a couple, to go through this to a good outcome, whatever that may be? Where can you get help?

◆ If you have kids together, how can their pain be minimised?

She doesn't know – Should you tell her?

You probably have a voice in you muttering *No, it would only hurt her.* Generally my advice is that the sooner you tell her what's happening the better, whether you're in an affair or merely burning with desire. Unless you have agreed to a sexually open relationship, you're abusing your partner and her trust in you if you keep her in ignorance.

I know it's not easy. In 1990, after eighteen years of marital fidelity, I had a brief affair when I was away on a week-long group in Scotland. Coming home, I was in emotional turmoil. It felt like all my credibility and my status as a trustworthy man who kept his promises were destroyed. It took me several weeks to find the courage to tell my wife. She was devastated, and it took many months to rebuild the trust. However, where a partner has been kept in ignorance for months or years, the trust may never be recovered.

Some years ago, I stayed for a few days with a friend of mine and his wife, let's call them Mark and Karen. One day, Karen took me aside and told me she had been having an affair for the past two years. She justified it by telling me how lousy Mark was as a lover and everything else. My sense was that Karen was expressing her anger at men in general by this affair, but she wasn't seeking my advice. My dilemma was whether to tell Mark, and I admit I chickened out. When he did find out, the damage was beyond repair, and the break-up was immediate. After a couple of years of sorting himself out, Mark is now happily remarried, whereas Karen has suffered from alcoholism and depression, and still has not faced her issues. If she had told Mark at the outset, *maybe* it could have turned out differently.

HANDLING A BIG BREAK-UP

When my marriage ended, my wife and I had been together for thirty years, since the age of twenty. After several years of struggle, it was my wife who insisted we had to finish. I was not surprised, but I was utterly devastated. It was like tearing a huge oak tree out by the roots. The effects of ending a long-term partnership will run through every part of your life: family, friends, home and your basic sense of who you are. It's also devastating financially.

Major separations rarely happen by complete mutual agreement. More often, one partner is pushing for it, and the other resisting. Sometimes one partner looks obviously to blame, by an affair, addictions and so on. Probably neither of you will have any precedent for this crisis, and your emotional and negotiating skills will be overwhelmed.

While one might hope that the instigator would be considerate and contrite towards their partner, often it's not so. Probably because they feel ashamed and don't have the skills to handle the situation, this partner can be almost unreachable, already off the picture and crazily impatient to finish the scene.

Whatever part you're playing in the drama, find as much compassion as you can for both of you, and go many extra miles to maintain some goodwill in your separation. If you have children together, cooperating amicably will make a massive difference to them and to both parents. Even if you don't, if you can end up with mutual goodwill and respect, you will be glad of it at some future stage.

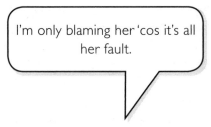

I'm only blaming her 'cos it's all her fault.

One of the reasons this is so traumatic is that you're probably facing a deep emotional crisis at the same time as negotiating on a complex mass of financial, legal and other matters, ranging from massive issues like divorce settlements and who keeps the house to equally massive questions like who gets the flat-screen TV and how you share the DVD collection. You need good support on all fronts: my best emotional support came from the men's group I had been part of for six years, which included a couple of men who had already been through similar crises. I was also lucky to be referred to an excellent divorce solicitor, who gave me some guidelines and urged me to minimise the fees by working out in commonsense terms with my wife the basics of a settlement.

If your partner is taking this hard, it will benefit both of you if you can help her to get some practical and emotional support. You may be feeling aggrieved and wanting to let her stew in her own juice, but it's better to swallow these feelings and be compassionate. If you have children, think about their support too. When my wife and I broke up, our daughters were eighteen and twenty, and I was unprepared for how hard they took it. Fortunately my parents stepped in and provided some of the steadiness we had lost from the family home.

Although blaming the other can soothe a wounded ego, the best books and counsellors believe it's never fair to blame one party entirely. There will be pay-offs for the other partner, like an excuse for righteous anger, and their behaviour will in some way collude with that of the 'guilty' party. If both of you can reach this level of understanding, it will help you reach forgiveness and goodwill. With children, if you can agree that neither partner will blame the other when explaining your break-up, all of you will benefit.

For more detailed guidance on handling the emotional impact of a break-up, see Chapter 2. Time for grieving is essential, but the best healing is achieved if the two of you can meet to celebrate all that was good between you, forgive each other face to face and complete. For more specific help on a big break-up, see Resources at the end of this chapter.

DATING SKILLS FOR MATURING MEN

I am sitting alone at a table for two in Galatea, the smartest of Glastonbury's informal eating places. Wearing smart casual gear which I hope looks youthful, I am waiting for my blind date, Jackie, to appear. To look my best, I am not wearing my glasses, which means that people entering the room are blurs to me. She looked good in the picture she sent me, but how long ago was that? A rather bulky female blur comes in, and I half rise, then sit back in relief. Now a slim and rather sexy female blur glides in, and I stand up. I've got it right – it is Jackie. As she gets closer, I realise she is wearing a gorgeous creamy, linen, semi-transparent trouser suit, and a sense of elation runs right through me.

Some years before this scene, I recall one of the single guys in my men's group telling me how he'd met this girl through a soul mates ad and had a blind date with her. It seemed scary and artificial to me, and I declared I'd never do it. In fact in my fifties, I had numerous blind dates through soul mates ads, and found two good relationships through them. But if you've been many years in one relationship, it's a strange new world to meet in midlife.

Here are some guidelines to get you started:

Make the best of yourself. If you've been living alone or in a long-term relationship, you may be used to scruffiness. When you're dating, you'll need smart, freshly washed clothes, a good shave and haircut, and fresh breath.

Screen before you date. Every blind date is a big emotional and time investment. Do as much screening as you can before meeting up to improve your chances of success. Know the kind of partner you are looking for and check things out by phone or email. Understand what *she* wants and if you're likely to suit her. Ask for a picture and send her yours. Learn what matters most to you and the questions that can explore this.

Enjoy the journey, not the outcome. Blind dates are nerve-wracking: you are both accepting or rejecting each other, and it probably happens within the first minute. I can recall a couple of blind dates with truly gorgeous women who ticked all my boxes, but were clearly not interested. There is a gift in all this: learning to value yourself even when she turns you down. I tried to enjoy the conversations, even when they were going nowhere.

Blind dates are not therapy sessions. If you're still hurting from a major break-up, this nice woman across the table may seem ideal to pour out your troubles to. Don't! Start with easy topics, go gradually deeper if it suits both of you. Keep it a dialogue: ask plenty of questions, talk about yourself, but not for too long. Talk about positives: what you enjoy, what you are looking for and what you can offer in a relationship.

Value what you offer. You may worry about your looks, but don't be hard on yourself. You're not in your twenties, that's just a fact. Fortunately, most mature women value other qualities more than looks. If you have learned Intimacy 101, if you offer emotional competence, empathy and dependability, you're a good prospect!

RELATIONSHIP PITFALLS: CO-DEPENDENCE, FLYING BOYS AND MORE

This is already a long chapter, so the aim of this section is to give a brief view of some of the major patterns which can block you from intimate relationships. I believe that most people develop a couple of dominating stories or patterns in childhood, which they repeat through adult life: relationships are a main arena in which these dramas are played out. But with determination, a wise partner, and some good processes and support, relationships can help in changing and healing these patterns.

Co-dependence

Co-dependence affects many people to some degree, and it's a complex condition which can take many forms – some deeply disruptive, some benign. I describe my 26-year marriage as a functional co-dependent relationship. In Resources you'll find the best books I've found on the topic. This section offers a snapshot to help you decide whether to dig further. Co-dependence is a situation where two people each require the other to behave in certain limited ways. These could range from angry to submissive: both partners are limited, distorted, partly suppressed by this arrangement, and it's unstable – if one person changes, there's no resilience to handle it.

Pia Mellody, an expert in this field, lists five symptoms of co-dependence:

1. Self-esteem either too low, over-inflated or based on external factors like money, possessions and children.

2. Difficulty setting boundaries with others: either too closed or too open (which leaves others feeling invaded).

3. Problems experiencing one's own reality, knowing who one is and sharing this with others.

4. Trouble knowing and meeting one's own needs and wants appropriately.

5. Lack of moderation in experiencing and expressing one's reality, ie extremes of emotions and behaviour.

Co-dependence can arise not only in primary partnerships, but in all relationships, including work and social. One model of how to progress beyond it suggests that the next stage is *independence*, where you pull back from dysfunctional connections and evolve beyond the symptoms above. Beyond this, the goal is *interdependence*: where you depend on others, and they on you, in appropriate ways which are not rigid or conditional, and can handle change. If you tell your partner, 'If you leave me, I'll die', that's co-dependent. If you tell her, 'If you leave me, I'd be deeply upset, but I would survive', that's interdependent.

Love Addicts, Avoidance Addicts and more

If you or your partner have addiction issues, it's bound to limit intimacy and hamper the relationship. A major addiction like alcoholism is likely to dominate both your lives. For more on addictions in general, see Chapter 7.

There is a linked pair of addictions which affect many relationships to some degree. Pia Mellody coined the terms *Love Addict* and *Avoidance Addict* to describe these patterns. The Love Addict is repeatedly drawn to the power and admiration which an Avoidance Addict offers: at first, the relationship with the Avoidance Addict brings relief from pain and emptiness, but as the Love Addict shows more of their neediness, the Avoidance Addict retreats, until eventually the Love Addict enters the painful phase of withdrawal, where despair, obsession and other symptoms are common. The cycle may repeat with the same partner or with a new Avoidance Addict.

The cycle for the Avoidance Addict is that they are attracted to the vulnerability of the Love Addict, and get a high from seducing them and meeting their needs for a while. Soon, the Avoidance Addict feels trapped and overwhelmed by the needs of the Love Addict, and abandons them. A period of withdrawal leads to a repeat of the cycle, with the same partner or a new one. Many people have these patterns to some degree and will be attracted to partners who play out the matching cycle. If this is affecting you, it's worth getting professional help and reading Pia's book on the subject (see Resources).

I have an Italian friend, Paolo, who is sexy and charming, and was an Avoidance Addict through his thirties and forties. He had a series of gorgeous girlfriends, but none lasted more than a few months, and he left a trail of broken hearts. Eventually he got into tantra (see more in Chapter 10) and broke the pattern. When I asked him how, Paolo said:

'You have to commit and just decide to stay with a relationship. I really thought I would die, so many times, it was so scary. I was not in control, I could not walk out. I was a little hurt child, and when she loved me like that, I started to be a real man for the first time.'

Flying Boys

This problem has several names. Carl Jung called it *Puer Aeternus* (*Perpetual Boy*), Robert Bly speaks of Flying Boys and Dan Kiley calls it Peter Pan Syndrome. All of them refer to men who are physically adults, but emotionally and mentally are children. They are liable to childish behaviour and emotional extremes, and have trouble handling adult responsibilities, including steady relationships. Sometimes they remain deeply attached to their mothers or look for a partner who will mother them.

As you may imagine, it's hard for men suffering this problem to identify and face it. If you are the partner of such a man, naming it may help you realise the scale of the problem. Bringing a man out of this towards maturity is typically a long and difficult process, which will need help from professionals and friends, as well as a very patient partner. As the partner, you need to decide if you are willing to accept sacrifices for his sake, and you need to test out if he is willing to try to change.

RESOURCES

Resources for this vital subject are grouped by sub-topic below, and some overlap, so look through all of them and choose the ones that suit you best. The communications and assertiveness skills will be valuable in many areas of your life.

Intimacy 101

I have tried over 100 writers about relationships, and Harville Hendrix is the best I've found. There's also a lot of useful information and tools on Harville's two websites: www.harville-hendrix.com and www.gettingtheloveyouwant.com.

Getting the Love You Want: A Guide for Couples, by Harville Hendrix. ISBN 978-0743495929. This will help you understand the basic dynamics of relationships, such as what attracts partners to each other. It has a good section on dealing with crises and a ten-step process for deepening intimacy, based on a series of excellent exercises which can be done over ten weeks.

Keeping the Love You Find: A Guide for Singles, by Harville Hendrix ISBN 978-0671734206. This is also excellent, with a set of well-grounded exercises to help you both understand and heal some of your wounds and negative patterns about relationships, and learn skills to start and sustain a more intimate relationship.

Loving Relationships, by Sondra Ray. ISBN 978-0890872444. Sondra is my second favourite writer on relationships. The style of this book is good for men because the chapters are brief, get straight to the point, and offer practical tools and checklists (eg 'Master the five biggies', 'Get clear on money') and emergency tips when you or your relationship is in crisis. If you work through this book, you will strengthen your intimacy skills, resilience and zest for love.

The Dance of Intimacy, by Harriet Goldhor Lerner. ISBN 978-0060916466. This book is subtitled *A Woman's Guide to Courageous Acts of Change in Key Relationships*, however, men can learn a lot from it, and there's no equivalent book for men. It gives a perceptive, practical view on many barriers to intimacy, such as the balance between self and relationship, boundaries and family dynamics.

Men Are from Mars, Women Are from Venus, by John Gray. ISBN 978-0007152599. I refused to read this for several years because the title sounded so corny. In fact, I found a lot of helpful wisdom for men and women, and ways to describe problems so that partners can talk about them.

I'm OK – You're OK, by Thomas A. Harris. ISBN 978-0099552413. This readable book is a popular classic in the self-help field. His key idea is that we each have a parent, adult and child aspect within us: this is a simple and powerful way to understand and improve communication problems in relationships of all kinds. He relates this to the games we all play, ie patterns of behaviour through which we avoid real dialogue and intimacy.

DIY Sex & Relationship Therapy, by Lori Boul. ISBN 978-1845284749. A delightfully clear, positive self-help book designed for couples to work through together. It has a cheerful, no-jargon approach and covers a range of key issues, including basic communication, handling conflicts and a good long section on sexual issues, including healing processes.

Communication skills and assertiveness

How to be Assertive in Any Situation, by Sue Hadfield and Gill Hasson. ISBN 978-0273738497. One of the most highly rated books on the topic. It provides a good grounding in communication and assertiveness skills for relationships and other situations.

Non-Violent Communication, by Marshall Rosenberg. ISBN 978-1892005038. A brilliant book: NVC is much more widely relevant than the name suggests. There are also excellent training groups and support networks based on NVC. See: www.liferesources.org.uk.

University Counselling Service: Although aimed at students, this is a sound introduction to the key skills of assertiveness for people of any age and has a good list of other books and resources. See: www.counselling.cam.ac.uk/assertiveness.

Co-counselling: A great way to learn and practise the skills of intimacy. You start by taking a Fundamentals training in basic methods of counselling and communication, eg expressing emotions, hearing them and clearing them. In co-counselling, you and another person take turns to counsel each other, with equal time for each person. After the initial training, you can access information about people in your area for ad-hoc sessions, local groups and residentials. See: www.co-counselling. info. The website explains what co-counselling is, what the training involves and offers excellent download material.

Helpguide.org: A good website for basic relationship skills, including topics like emotional intelligence, and understanding anger and conflict resolution. Their Emotional Skills Toolkit is also good. See: www.helpguide.org/topics/relationships.htm.

Renewing the long-term partnership

The best book to help you with this is *Getting the Love You Want*, by Harville Hendrix (see above).

Better Relationships, by Sarah Litvinoff. ISBN 978-0091856700. Published by Relate, this is a good basic guide to relationship dynamics, including the challenges of long-term relationships.

Staying Together, by Susan Quilliam. ISBN 978-0091856717. This is specifically about how to face a relationship which is failing and how to take stock and overcome difficulties.

College of Sexual and Relationship Therapists: For professional help, see www.cosrt.org.uk or try the Counselling Directory at www.counselling-directory.org.

The Danger Zone: Affairs

Affairs: A Guide to Working Through the Repercussions of Infidelity, by Emily Brown. ISBN 978-1118493601. Written by one of the American experts in this field, it is a really good, practical book, including understanding an affair, learning the lessons and working through the consequences, whether the couple stay together or separate.

The Relate Guide to Starting Again, by Sarah Litvinoff. ISBN 978-0091856670. A shorter, simpler, British book which can also guide you through the process of resolving an affair and moving on.

Affairs-Help: Emily Brown's website has a useful self-assessment questionnaire, advice on getting help, and a good list of books and relevant websites. See: www.affairs-help.com.

Netdoctor: A simple, short, commonsense overview of the topic, with useful links for further information. See: www.netdoctor. co.uk/affairs.

Relate: Relate is the largest UK provider of relationship support. The website has helpful, basic advice and can put you in touch with a local Relate counsellor or telephone and online counselling. See: www.relate.org.uk.

College of Sexual and Relationship Therapists: For professional help, see www.cosrt.org.uk or try the Counselling Directory at www.counselling-directory.org or Relate at www.relate.org.uk.

Handling a big break-up

The Good Divorce, by Constance Ahrons. ISBN 978-0060926342. A valuable guide to handling a break-up without permanent damage to the partners or the family. It's also good on how to cope if your partner is withdrawn or hostile.

How to Have a Healthy Divorce, by Paula Hall. ISBN 978-0091924003. Good on handling the emotions, finding personal support and creating an action plan for moving on.

Divorce and Splitting Up: A Complete Legal and Financial Guide, by Claire Colbert. ISBN 978-1844900671. A thorough guide to the UK legal and financial practicalities, including sections on cohabiting couples, maintenance, differences in Scotland and Northern Ireland and how to minimise legal costs by drafting agreements yourself.

Counselling Directory: For specialist counsellors, you will find a section on separation and divorce specialists at www.counsel-ling-directory.org.

Dating skills for maturing men

The best resources for this situation are listed in Intimacy 101 above. And remember Mark Twain's advice, '*The best way to learn fast is to make a lot of mistakes in a short space of time*'. Enjoy!

Relationship pitfalls: Codependence, Flying Boys and more

Facing codependence, by Pia Mellody. ISBN 978-0062505897. A thorough explanation of the symptoms and causes of codependence. However, the section on recovery is only twelve pages long, so you might prefer to go straight to the workbook below.

Breaking Free: A Recovery Workbook for Facing Codependence, by Pia Mellody and others. ISBN 978-0062505903. A good, long, heavy-duty process for understanding and clearing the underlying causes of codependence, which are typically childhood issues. It is advisable to get professional support with this process.

Facing Love Addiction: Giving Yourself the Power to Change the Way You Love, by Pia Mellody. ISBN 978-0062506047. This gives a clear explanation about these two addictive patterns of behaviour and how they play out with each other. It has extensive sections on the process of recovering from either of these patterns, including keeping a journal and other self-help processes, plus a good chapter on the qualities of a healthy relationship.

The Secret Lives of Men, by Christopher Blazina. ISBN 978-0757306600. This is an engaging book, helpful on a lot of men's issues and includes chapters on the Flying Boy and the Lost Boy. He makes good use of movie characters to illustrate his ideas.

The Flying Boy: Why Men Run from Relationships, by John Lee. ISBN 978-1558740068. One of the few available books on this topic.

Chapter 4

Work, money – and fulfilment

Your work is going to fill a large part of your life, and the only way to be truly satisfied is to do what you believe is great work. And the only way to do great work is to love what you do. If you haven't found it yet, keep looking. Don't settle. As with all matters of the heart, you'll know when you find it.

STEVE JOBS

Many men still have a deep-rooted sense that success means competing and achieving, especially in work. The measures of this success are narrow: fame, money, business empires. They rarely last long, and few achieve them. But work matters deeply to most men: it gives a feeling of self-worth and identity, for yourself, and your family and friends. It's also an important source of social contact and support.

Men run a big risk of thinking their work is who they are. I recall Nick, on a weekend group, who was a high-flyer through his thirties and forties, and then burned out and started working part-time. He said, 'I used to think I was nothing without a posh car, and at least six grand a month. These days I'm working for a charity, earning peanuts, but I'm getting a huge income of satisfaction, seeing what I can do for someone else'.

These days, when you're fifty, you may have twenty or thirty good working years ahead of you – potentially. But most organisations bring people to career peaks in their forties and can't adjust to the vintage, maturing years. That's just one of the work issues for men beyond fifty. Here are some more:

◆ Feeling stuck, stale and demotivated in your work.

◆ Facing redundancy or retirement: sometimes chosen, sometimes imposed.

◆ Handling the new demands and potential isolation of self-employment.

◆ Feeling passed over, outshone, and unvalued by the organisation and younger high-flyers.

◆ Frustration or depression because you want to do something worthwhile but can't see how.

There are also money issues in this life stage, explored later in the chapter. You probably have new financial priorities, like funding retirement, health care, ageing parents or a divorce when the scope to earn good money seems to be shrinking. So your work choices have to match your money needs, but look at fulfilment first and finance second.

What this chapter offers is some new approaches to assess what work means for you, tools to find a new vision and try it out, pointers on handling self-employment, redundancy and retirement, and ways to look anew at money and managing it.

WORK: SOME NEW PERSPECTIVES

Many men would no more think about work than a fish would think about water: it's just there, you have to swallow it every day. But if you want to make changes in your life, work can be a good place to start: you can't alter your family and your history, but you probably have more freedom about work choices than you believe – especially if you reduce your financial pressures.

To help you loosen assumptions and open to fresh options, here are six useful ways of looking at your work.

1. From careers to portfolios

Charles Handy is one of the few management gurus who brings the worlds of feeling and inspiration to this area. He was among the first to predict the huge changes in our ways of working in the past twenty years, and he coined the term portfolio working. He suggests that work is like savings: it's unwise to invest everything in one place. The notion of a linear career, a steady progression in one line of work from school leaver to gold watch at sixty-five, is pretty obsolete, but what's to replace it?

Handy suggests that we think of work as any activity with a productive output, and aim for a portfolio of work, so we have diverse sources of income and satisfaction. This should also mean that if one piece of our work portfolio disappears, we're not up the creek. In his book, *The Age of Unreason*, he writes of five types of work for the portfolio:

◆ *Wage work. Where money is paid for time inputs.*

◆ *Fee work. Where money is paid for results delivered. This is more typical of self-employment, growing rapidly especially as more jobs are outsourced.*

◆ *Homework. Includes cleaning, repairs, caring for kids or parents: rarely paid, but still vital.*

◆ *Gift work. Voluntary, unpaid work helping others, eg in your local community.*

◆ *Study work. Includes training and learning for new skills: growing in popularity as change speeds up.*

One great benefit of looking at your work as a portfolio is that you have several choices to consider, not just one. You probably have various needs from your work, such as money, social contact, learning and fulfilment, and you may look to different parts of your portfolio to fulfil these. Handy believes the idea of retirement has become obsolete, and I agree with him: the portfolio makes it easier to see your work as a transition across time. As you get into your sixties and seventies, you may no longer have the energy, desire or financial need to spend as much time earning money, but you'll probably still want a work portfolio of some kind.

2. Repeating patterns at work

Through the 1990s, I led many workshops on how to fulfil yourself at work, mostly for men. One surprising thing was how often men play out the same repeating patterns in work as in relationships and other parts of their lives. If you had a bullying, angry father who said you were never good enough, you will probably find this experience repeated in your bosses, business partners or even colleagues. Changing your work, or your approach to it, is one of the better ways to shift such patterns, and the change can then spread to other parts of your life.

Consider the major setbacks, frustrations and upsets you feel about your work currently and in the past. Are there some repeating patterns, scenarios or emotions that keep coming round? Can you relate these to crucial episodes in your childhood? You may want to consider counselling or therapy to clear the original feelings. But also look at how you can change things in your work so that the old patterns are no longer stirred up in you.

3. Dangerous role models (Or 'He's not the Messiah, he's a very naughty boy')

Look at the impossible expectations we place upon our leaders in politics, sport, business and beyond, and ask yourself where did this all start? We expect our leaders and heroes to be superpowerful, super-ethical and self-sacrificing. Sooner or later it becomes clear that every leader and hero is human, has faults, and another crucifixion by media results. It's not a healthy set of expectations, whether you are leading or being led.

> **Blaming the leader is much easier than blaming yourself.**

The insight here is to be aware and careful about the role models that you and people around you buy into: especially if you are a leader or a manager, since the chances are that sometime you will have a painful fall. It helps to realise that this is a repeating pattern, which our culture, led by the news media, plays out time and again. If you can value yourself and the opinion of a few close friends, it may give you some resilience if you get caught up in this pattern. You could also look back at the section on role models in Chapter 1 and choose some fresh role models for your work.

4. Human sustainability at work

The basics of environmental sustainability are familiar to most of us, such as balancing energy inputs and output, using renewable energy sources and recycling. Organic farming produces food sustainably: have you ever thought that these same principles of sustainability and organic growth could apply to people and the way they live and work? My first book, *The Natural Advantage: Renewing Yourself*, grew from my experience of starting an organic farm, and it translates the methods of organic growth to people and their work. For example, clean energy sources for your work are enthusiasm and inspiration, whereas pressure, fear and stress are like artificial fertilisers which force the growth but pollute your underlying resources. See more on this in Chapter 11.

Adopting the organic approach can help individuals and whole organisations work in a way which renews their human resources, instead of depleting and polluting them, and brings more fulfilment. To give you a practical taste of this approach, try doing the Personal Energy Audit in Appendix 1. Many people have used this process to see if their work is humanly sustainable. You can also use it to assess any new line of work you are considering.

5. Left side, right side: Using your full brain

Think about your own life and those of other men you admire: how often are logic and analysis the keys to success? Mostly it's vision, intuition and gut feel, which come from the right side of the brain. Nobel Prize-winning research by Sperry and Ormstein identified the different skills of the left and right hemispheres of the brain. What we usually regard as thinking and brain skills come from the left side of the brain: analysis, structure and so on. Most men rely too much on these left-brain skills and have trouble linking them to the vital gifts of the right side, such as imagination, intuition and synthesis – seeing new solutions and meaning in a messy, complex situation.

One of the most basic skills maturing men need in reinventing themselves is to access the right side of the brain as a guide instead of attacking every problem with the left: the left side of the brain is a great executive but a lousy leader. You can find tools to access these right-brain skills in Resources and Appendix 1. Re-visioning your work is a great place to try them out.

6. You can get it if you really want it...

A lot of maturing men feel powerless and unhappy about work: whether they have some or not. Those in work are often unfulfilled and unappreciated, but believe it's too late to change. Those without work fear they're too old to be employable. Work offers huge scope for most men of any age to change, grow, learn and have adventures, especially if you accept that not all work has to be paid and that you *can* reduce any money pressures. I've had plenty of pleasure and fulfilment from work beyond fifty, and many other men have too. So, believe it's possible and use the next section to help you.

RE-VISIONING YOUR WORK

This section is unlike most in the book, since it offers a sequence of self-guided processes to help you understand what you want and need from your work, find a new vision of fulfilling yourself and explore practical steps to make it a reality. To make best use of this sequence, set aside two or three hours to work through the main exercises in order: don't skim them beforehand or you'll lose their effect. The whole sequence uses the Diamond Process described in detail in my first book, *The Natural Advantage*. This has three main steps, which integrate the analytical and creative sides of the brain. Sections A), B) and C) below show how to apply this sequence to re-visioning your work. Although this process is designed for re-visioning your work, you can adapt it to many parts of your life.

A) Firstly, use left-brain skills of analysis and logic to explore and understand more deeply your needs, blind spots and future hopes.

1. *Personal Energy Audit.* If you haven't done the Personal Energy Audit in Appendix 1, do it now. It offers valuable insights about work–life balance: what you are really putting into, and getting out of, your work. In reviewing your Audit, highlight *three* aspects of work that you'd really like to change for the future.

2. *Timeframe and future needs.* Choose a forward time horizon for your re-visioning. This might be anything from six months to sixteen years. For example, if you have just suffered a major shipwreck in your life, such as redundancy or major illness, you may set a short timeframe in which you can recover your balance and gently explore future options. Once you've set your time period, think about your needs during it: for example, do you want to relocate, do you need to save money for a pension or care costs, do you want to reduce working time to leave space for something new?

3. *Working highs and lows.* Don't rush this one: it can give you crucial insights into what you do and don't want from your work in future. Recall three events or periods when you were really happy and fulfilled in your work, and three when you

were dejected and dissatisfied. Take time to recall each of these in some detail: let yourself get right back into the feelings you had at the time. For the highs, analyse why this event or period was so good for you – for example, were you using your talents to the full, were you enjoying a lot of contact with congenial colleagues, were you getting kudos and recognition...

Make some notes of what has really given you fulfilment in work in the past: this is a good test of any future options. Analyse the difficult times and what you may want to change in yourself or avoid around you in your future work.

4. *Elusive dreams.* Let yourself freewheel, relax and recall any daydreams or wild ideas you've had about the kind of work you'd love to do. As a child, what did you dream of doing as a grown-up? When you were doing exams as a teenager, did you have hopes of where this was heading? In your twenties or thirties, did you have a grand plan that never came to pass? Don't judge or criticise any of these crazy dreams, just enjoy them and see what particular satisfactions they would have given you.

B) Now relax and let your intuition and creativity envision a way to meet your varying needs and overcome the constraints.

This is where you call upon your intuition. It's important to do this section when you're feeling relaxed and in a congenial place. If possible, go for a walk and find a peaceful spot to sit, or arrange a quiet hour or two at home. During these processes, imagine your intuition is one of the various voices within you, and actually call upon it, ask for its best guidance at this important decision point in your life.

1. *Fantasy ticket.* This is the second exercise in Appendix 1. A vital part of this process is exploring the fantasy and seeing what it means to you: make sure you do this before moving on to Section C).

2. *Work-life vision statement.* This is the third exercise in Appendix 1. Go through this process in sequence, then spend some time sitting with your statement, seeing how you feel about it and considering where it could lead you.

As you do these two exercises and as you review the results, suspend judgement and analysis – these come later. Let yourself get excited and enjoy fresh vision.

> **'There are only two tragedies in life: one is not getting what one wants, and the other is getting it.'**
> *Oscar Wilde*

C) Use the left brain again to devise practical ways in which you can make your new vision a practicality.

Fantasy to reality? By this stage, you may have a big idea, a vision which is exciting and scary. The inner critic may be shouting in your ear, *'Back off, you fool! This will never work, and anyway, you're too old for this'*. I have worked with many men in this delicate stage of holding a vision that could mean a lot, and feeling self-doubt, practical worries and fearing the reaction of those around them. There are ways to test-drive your fantasy. You don't have to jump off a cliff – find the steps. This third section doesn't need to be done all in one go and there may be benefits in having a break, leaving time for some intuition and coming back to it several times.

1. *The eight-six-three reality filter.* This is Exercise 4 in Appendix 1. It will ask you to set some action goals and timings for yourself. Be realistic about the goals and really try to achieve them.

2. *Yeses and buts: Inner and outer dialogues.* By now, you hopefully have a voice within that's inspired and excited about a possible new work direction. You may also have a doubtful, critical voice which feels you're getting above yourself and throws up loads of practical objections. As you start to share your idea with people

around you, you may find these yes and but voices are also carried by some of them.

Invite the two inner voices to debate the subject: find another voice within you, maybe the Wise Elder, who can guide the debate and help resolve it. Also try having the outer dialogue: ask two or three people close to you to have a similar debate, where you just observe. These dialogues can help you understand what you really want, see which practical objections are important and how to move forward.

3. *Backcasting.* This technique can be really useful in many areas of your life. The basic idea is to start from the end result and then figure out how you got there. See Exercise 5 in Appendix 1.

4. *Seven pearls of practical wisdom.* This is not an exercise but a list of good methods to use as you explore how to move from fantasy to reality.

(a) *Networking.* Once you have a list of practical steps and information needs, use your networks of friends and contacts as fully as possible. Remember it's not just about the people you know, it's about the people *they* know too. For a detailed guide on how to use focused networking in a work setting, read the book *What Colour is Your Parachute?* (see Resources).

(b) *Volunteering.* Among the many people I have helped with their work, this has been one of the most successful tactics. Right now, you may lack experience and skills for the work you want to do, but there's a good chance that by volunteering you can gain them. Charities and non-profit bodies are often a good start, since they are used to working with semi-skilled volunteers, and should provide some support and training.

(c) *Find role models.* Use your own networking, plus web searches, online forums and book searches to identify people who have made a similar work move to the one you hope for. As a minimum, read about their experience and, ideally, ask to meet them.

(d) *Training.* Whether or not you need to learn specific skills for a new area of work, training courses can be a good move. They normally offer scope for work experience and advice on how to find paid work in this field. They should also open up more contacts, and give you extra confidence and credibility.

(e) *Temporary positions.* You might find these by offering to provide short-term cover in an organisation or by approaching temp agencies. Even if the pay is meagre, it will give you experience which is a useful credential, and help you decide whether this line of work is really for you.

(f) *Shadow or gofer.* These days, it's quite common for secondary school students to have a week or two of unpaid work as a shadow or junior assistant in a work organisation which interests them. You may feel odd about asking for this at your mature age, but why not try?

(g) *Have a plan, get a buddy.* It can be painful to face the uncertainty of whether your dream can happen: sometimes it's easier to rubbish the dream and forget it. Having a plan and reviewing it often can help you: give yourself a few modest targets at first and a sensible timeframe. Find a buddy who can remind you of the goals you set, celebrate the progress and support you in any setbacks.

ENJOYING YOUR DAILY WORK

Hopefully you have found work which you believe will be fulfilling and can match your vision. Remember the portfolio idea described earlier: work can include volunteering and studying, as well as paid work. Actually enjoying your work day to day is a different challenge. A lot of work organisations are pretty exhausting and inhuman. And your own negative beliefs can play out at work too. It's *very* easy to get lost in the daily demands of a job and to forget why you're here. Try to remind yourself of three needs and review whether you're meeting them:

◆ *Your own needs.* You may have several different needs, such as money, social contact and using your talents. The processes earlier in the chapter should help you be clear about what you need.

◆ *What the organisation or project needs.* Especially if this is paid work, stay aware of what you're being paid for, but recognise that what the organisation actually needs may differ from your official job description: for example, you may play a vital role in the emotional wellbeing of the team or as a sounding board for the boss's new ideas, but you also have to deliver on your official tasks.

◆ *Other people at work.* If you can work in a climate of mutual support and companionship, it will be more fun and you're more likely to get help when you're in a hole. Even if the organisation culture seems competitive, create a good atmosphere among those you work with and treat others as you would like them to treat you. Appreciation and celebration lift most people's spirits.

For bigger insights and more advice on all the topics in this section, try two books in Resources. One is *Seven Habits of Highly Effective People* by Stephen Covey: an international bestseller by a well-known management guru, strong on the human, emotional and spiritual aspects of work, and on practical ways to organise yourself. The other is my first book, *The Natural Advantage: Renewing Yourself*, which shows how both the principles and practices of organic growth can be translated to people and organisations.

I have set out below some brief pointers on ways to enjoy your daily work, avoid common pitfalls and learn from the problems. If you're in a highly stressful job, this may seem naively optimistic. Many people find their work tough, there are often pressures which squeeze the fun out of work, but I stand by my view that you can enjoy it!

◆ *Believe in pleasure.* Remember the story of Tinkerbell in *Peter Pan:* what you believe has a big influence on what happens. *Believing* that it's possible to enjoy your work, and that you deserve to have fun and fulfilment, is a vital prelude to it happening.

◆ *Check your beliefs.* Use Exercise 6 in Appendix I to see if you still have negative beliefs about work which limit your potential to enjoy it. If so, make clearing and healing these beliefs a priority.

◆ *Get organised.* Most people have never learned basic skills like time-management and setting priorities, which can make a massive difference to how effectively you work, and your ability to get results and satisfaction without working crazy hours. Stephen Covey's book is excellent for this.

◆ *Use the learning opportunities.* It can be easier to learn new skills and experiment in your work than other parts of your life, such as family or relationships. Many of the relationship skills described in Chapter 3, such as assertiveness, listening skills and conflict resolution, can help you in your work, and it's a great place to try them out.

◆ *Use the difficulties.* You may be doing a task, working in a team, coping with a boss, that are undeniably stressful. Instead of feeling like a powerless victim of such situations, believe you've chosen them for your own learning and growth. You could even treat them as a spiritual path to see if you can stay centred and contribute positively in an abrasive context.

◆ *Draw the line if you have to.* I'm not suggesting you should continue indefinitely in work that's proving difficult. At the extreme, you may be in a situation which is actually abusive or unhealthy, or your unhappiness may just be a sign that it's time to move on. So be willing to tell an employer what's wrong, set deadlines and walk away if you have to.

◆ *Create companionship.* Look for mutual support and a real sense of fellowship, ideally with a whole team, or at least with one or two colleagues. You may have more awareness and skills to improve things than the people you are working with.

◆ *Keep renewing yourself.* It's very easy to get depleted by your work and to lose awareness that it's happening. Do the Personal Energy Audit in Appendix 1 regularly and use the methods in *The Natural Advantage.*

HOW TO ENJOY GOING SELF-EMPLOYED

Whether you're jumping into self-employment or being pushed by outside forces, it's a fact that the percentage of men who are self-employed and not on someone's payroll grows strongly through the forties, fifties and sixties. I was forty-two when I left my well-salaried job, handed back the company Jaguar and sat at home alone with the answerphone. I've enjoyed the freedom of being self-employed, but there are downsides, especially the risk of isolation.

I know many men who are literally one-man bands: it's hard to sustain your morale and motivation over a long period with no colleagues and work mates, especially if your business hits problems. There are ways to work with others on a self-employed basis. For example, you could be a sub-contractor to a small team or a large organisation. You won't get such benefits as paid holidays or pensions, but you have the freedom to walk away when it suits you. This kind of set-up not only gives you some social contact, but can mean you don't have to learn skills you don't want to, such as selling your services or IT. After six months of working on my own, I realised that I needed to work with people, and that the training and consulting work I wanted to do required a team with a bigger range of skills than I could offer. I became an Associate of a management consultancy near me, which meant that I could work as part of their team, but was free to do my own work in parallel.

If you're considering self-employment, here are some pointers to help you enjoy it:

◆ *Plan before you jump.* It's far less stressful if you can build up your contacts, skills and finances while you're on someone's payroll than when you're out on your own and have to pay the bills every month. If you know the direction you want to go, you can probably do some of this legitimately as part of your current job, or else in your spare time.

◆ *Lower your break-even.* This is explored in the Money section below. Try to cut your monthly outgoings and so reduce the minimum income you need to earn when you are self-employed.

◆ *Look for baseload income.* This means finding a steady source of income, probably part-time, which covers your break-even expenses and means you don't need to worry if your self-employed freelance earnings build up slowly. One friend of mine trained as a psychotherapist in his forties, and when he left his paid work in market research, he got a long-term contract to work two days a week as a student counsellor with a university. Jobs like this are out there and you might find such part-time work on an employed basis.

◆ *Figure out the sales and marketing.* If your type of self-employed work needs a steady stream of new clients and contacts, you'll probably find that one-third of your time is taken up in prospecting – making new contacts, writing proposals, promoting yourself via social media and having exploratory meetings. You need to understand this aspect of self-employment and either embrace it gladly or consider alternatives. Becoming a sub-contractor to a bigger organisation is one good option. Sometimes you can find individuals or agencies that sell for you and you pay for each new client they generate.

◆ *Have some savings before you start.* Being self-employed is pretty insecure. You can't control the flow of customers, let alone health problems, recessions and credit crunches. Try to start with a financial cushion: not only for the early period, but also to help if you hit a lean patch later.

◆ *Know and meet your social needs.* For many men, work is a major source of social contacts. Be clear what you need and how you can meet this when you are self-employed. There may be local networking groups you can join, or find congenial people who you can set up with as a partnership or small team. Managing these working relationships can sometimes be difficult, but a team has more capacity, skills and resilience than any one-man band.

◆ *A cunning plan.* Whatever your line of work, it's crucial to have a business plan. Finance is one vital part of this: it also needs to include sales and marketing, skills training, any certifications you need and lots more. Ask one or two competent friends to be a sounding board for your plan. And if this stuff is not your forte, there are books and websites, or you could look for a helpful accountant – they do exist!

◆ *Remember your vision.* You may know the saying, 'When you are up to your neck in alligators, it's hard to remember that you came here to drain the swamp'. Hopefully, you have a vision that excites you about going self-employed. Keep in touch with that spark of inspiration. Have a review every six or twelve months: one friend of mine doing pioneering work in holistic health care had an annual half day review with me and another professional to review his progress towards the vision and make sure he did not lose himself in the daily details.

HANDLING RETIREMENT OR REDUNDANCY

These words may sound threatening, but they don't need to be. The removal of the compulsory retirement age leaves individuals with a lot more choice. Although the idea of redundancy may sound only one better than cancer, the actuality can be pretty positive. Many men have taken voluntary redundancy to leave a job where they were stagnating and made a fresh start. Whether you've chosen redundancy or retirement, or had it imposed on you, there are emotional impacts, practicalities and new choices to consider. Let's look at each of these in turn.

Emotional impact

Leaving a job and a work team is a loss and a kind of bereavement, even if you chose to leave and even if you weren't enjoying the job. There will be a hole in your daily life where work and colleagues used to be. Give yourself time to adjust and process it, let yourself grieve and also celebrate, hopefully with the colleagues you're saying goodbye to. The material on grieving in Chapter 2 could be useful.

You may feel excited or nervous about having a big space open up in your life. Having freedom of choice can be hard, especially if you're not used to it. It's striking that many men suffer depression, ill health or addictions *after* they leave work. So recognise that this could be a difficult time and prepare for it:

◆ Create a bit of structure, at least for a transitional period: for example, sign up for a weekly adult education class, do one day a week of volunteering or join a regular sports group.

◆ Schedule a few treats in case your mood needs lifting: a holiday, an outing or a visit to friends.

◆ Make sure you have a good network of friends, so you have mates to talk to and go out with and support in case you need it. If you don't have many friends outside your work, try to change this before you leave: use some of the methods from Chapter 9.

◆ Stopping work may create free time that fills up with depression or worry about both past and future. If so, get help: see Chapters 2 and 7.

Another emotional impact may be in your relationship. One way or another, the dynamics are likely to change when you have more free time and are probably at home a lot more. This is not always a good thing for the relationship: you need to have some honest talks with your partner about her hopes and fears for the new phase, and yours. If she's still working full-time, does she expect you to keep house? Or does she hope you'll spend most of your free time together?

You may be shocked to find that you and your partner have different ideas about this new era. Try to find ways of meeting some of her hopes and yours. For example, plan to do some new things together, but also give yourself space, and if you need some peace and quiet, negotiate ways to get it. Don't replace your old boss with your partner!

Practicalities

Both retirement and redundancy are major financial events: it's important for your stress levels to look at this before you stop work and go through the implications with a professional financial advisor. Make sure that the process has been handled correctly by your employer and that you're getting your entitlements. For example, an employer is usually required to consult with workers before any redundancies. Another important practicality is knowing what State benefits you may be entitled to after you stop work. These are complex fields, where you may need to spend some time researching them yourself or getting help. See Resources for more on this.

New starts

Looking back over the decades of your working life, have you enjoyed them most of the time or have they been a dull blur? Do you feel you made good choices or bad ones about the work you did? Or maybe no choices because you were a helpless victim of fate at every turn? Your beliefs are crucial to your future: if you believe you make lousy choices or always end up unhappy in your work, you probably expect the same in future.

If you're carrying this kind of emotional baggage along with you, invest some time in reshaping your beliefs and freeing up your future. The material in several earlier chapters of the book can help you. Once you feel you're no longer blinkered or burdened by these negative beliefs, use the re-visioning process earlier in this chapter. I share Charles Handy's view that we never really stop work, we just change the forms it takes. And embracing the idea of working for little or no money can be really liberating: for a start, it makes you think what else you might want to receive for the energy you put out!

GETTING CLEAR WITH MONEY

Do you have issues around money? Most of us do. And as with work, your problem with money may be a symptom of some deeper habit or belief. Money is such a big thing in our lives that your attitude to money may mirror basic beliefs about yourself. For example, if you often feel short of money, does this reflect a belief that no one values you, you're not good enough or you have to struggle for everything? Do you have problems about money in your relationships or with your boss? Dig deeper to see what it's really about: perhaps you are competing to get enough love, power or recognition, and finance is simply the currency you're measuring with. Although your money symptoms, like serious lack of it, may look bad, don't start here: use the money pressures to get down to root causes, clear the old emotions, and change the negative habits and beliefs.

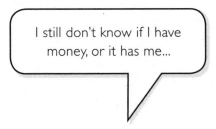

I still don't know if I have money, or it has me...

Peter Koenig, one of the best teachers on money I know, says there are far more taboos on disclosures about money than about sex in our culture. Think of your friends and work colleagues: you probably know a lot more about their personal life than you do about their money. In my men's group, it felt like a bold breakthrough when we actually told each other what income and capital we had. Because of these taboos, you may not have much awareness of your beliefs and habits about money. Use Exercise 7 in Appendix 1 to help you at this stage.

One common belief about money is poverty consciousness: a sense that there isn't enough money to go round, that you don't deserve to have much. Maybe you believe it's morally wrong to have money, or you shouldn't be richer than your parents, or having money will provoke jealousy and hostility from others. This may link to believing you're a victim, at the mercy of outside events and other people, that you can never get enough of whatever you need – money, love and more.

There are also people who struggle with having wealth, who feel guilty because they have more than others, who don't know how to balance spending on themselves with giving money to help the starving millions and the rainforest. Whatever your emotional baggage about money, invest time to lighten the load. You need to reach a stage where your decisions about money are led by clear thinking and a code of values you've chosen, not by floods of muddy feeling. When you believe you're getting towards this level of clarity, use the practical tips below.

Practical tips on money

These really are tips on a very large iceberg of information. See Resources for lots more.

◆ *Lower your break-even.* This means reducing your outgoings so that the minimum monthly income you need is less. Ways to do this include moving to a smaller house so you free up capital or reduce your rent or borrowings; paying off other debts, especially credit cards; making lifestyle choices which mean you spend less, such as UK cycling holidays not flights to the tropics; or selling your car and joining a car club. There are several benefits to this strategy: one is that you have more freedom and power of choice, since you don't need so much income. And a less expensive lifestyle will almost certainly be more environmentally sustainable.

◆ *Plan how to meet your long-term money needs.* Take a thorough look at your needs and wants for money through to the end of your life and plan how you are going to meet them. You may need more information and expert help to do this, but it's up to you to take the initiative and ensure it's done well. Include in this plan provisions for medical costs and residential or home care.

◆ *Understand your future income sources.* The pension field is complex, but you need to know what should be coming to you from pensions and other investments. Although it's a delicate subject, clarify if you're likely to inherit money from your parents or others.

◆ *Shop around for good advice.* Finding impartial, objective financial guidance is hard. Many advisors, even those who seem independent, may have ties or bonus payments that distort their advice. You need to invest time to find the good advice you need: ask friends, do a web search and interview at least three potential advisors. And ask direct questions about how they make their money, what happens to commissions on investments they recommend, and so on. Beware of 'magic bullet' money-making schemes which seem too good to be true: they are!

◆ *Review your investments and arrangements regularly.* Markets, taxation and your needs can all change fast. Even if you find this stuff complex, review the performance of your savings and update your plans at least annually, with an advisor.

◆ *Plan ahead for family needs.* The biggest may be providing for your wife or partner in case you die first. There are some simple steps which help, like putting assets in joint names, and an accountant or solicitor can advise on these. You may feel you're not providing enough: do what you can and talk it through openly with your partner. If she is worried, you could decide jointly to save money now to provide more.

◆ *Know what's happening to your money.* Understand what your savings are actually invested in. Who is managing them and how, what standards they operate to and who's making money from this process. Realise that you have choices, such as using ethical investments: this means screening to avoid investments in companies making arms or tobacco, for example.

• *Balance your needs and the bigger picture.* Try to find a fair balance in allocating your spending among different demands. You want to live comfortably, but can you share some of your income to meet the needs of other people or the many problems we have on our planet? In doing so, don't just give money away blindly: have some connection with the people or projects you are helping.

RESOURCES

For topics around work, retirement and redundancy, it's worth doing a web search as there may be new websites and changes in funding arrangements.

Work: perspectives, re-visioning, enjoying

The 7 Habits of Highly Effective People, by Stephen Covey. ISBN 978-0684858395. This combines a lot of clear, practical thinking with strong human values. It should make your work more pleasurable as well as more effective. There's a summary of the book and other resources at www.stephencovey.com.

The Natural Advantage: Renewing Yourself, by Alan Heeks. ISBN 978-1857882612. This uses the principles and practices of organic growth to show how people and organisations can combine achieving results with fulfilment and a way of working that is renewing, not depleting. There's a summary of the key ideas at www.thenaturaladvantage.com.

The Age of Unreason, by Charles Handy. ISBN 978-0099548317. Charles Handy is one of the most perceptive writers about the world of work and its relationship to human needs, including the search for meaning, and the immense changes coming from technology and economic pressures. This book introduces the portfolio concept mentioned in Chapter 4, along with Boiled Frog syndrome and more. Several of Handy's books have useful insights about work: for example, *The Empty Raincoat* (ISBN 978-0099301257) has a section on the issues of what he calls the Third Age, which is the life stage of maturing men.

What Color is Your Parachute?, by Richard Bolles. ISBN 978-1607741473. This is subtitled *A Practical Manual for Job-Hunters and Career-Changers*, and it delivers just that. There's also lots of free information and guidance on www.jobhuntersbible.com.

Going self-employed

If you try a Google search, you will get millions of listings in this area. Here are a few which may help you get started:

PRIME: This is the Prince's Initiative for Mature Enterprise, specifically aimed at helping those over fifty into self-employment. You can access good briefing material through the Prime Business Club, and potentially make networking contacts and find a mentor to help you get started. See: www.primebusiness-club.com.

Adviceguide: A useful website created by Citizen's Advice for a range of situations. If you search on self-employment, there is a checklist of practical issues, with links to further information. See: www.adviceguide.org.uk.

Business Link: At the time of writing, the UK Government still offers help for small businesses, including the self-employed, and you can access some of this through www.businesslink.gov.uk.

Going Self-Employed: How to Start Out in Business on Your Own – and Succeed!, by Steve Gibson. ISBN 978-0716021889. A useful, readable manual which covers most of the practicalities, including such issues as sales and marketing.

Be Your Own Boss: Teach Yourself, by Matt Avery. ISBN 978-1444111842. Another good guide, covering some of the human issues like self-confidence as well as the logistical ones.

Handling retirement or redundancy

The website www.redundancyexpert.co.uk is a good place to start on many aspects of redundancy: for example, it can brief you about your employer's obligations, how to fight a redundancy, what benefits you are entitled to and also handling depression. The website and blog at www.expertcareers.co.uk has useful material on a range of work-related topics, including redundancy.

Brilliant Retirement, by Nic Pelling. ISBN 978-0273723271. Subtitled *Your Practical Guide to a Happy, Healthy, Financially Sound Retirement*, it does what it says on the cover: it addresses all the issues highlighted in my short section in more depth, plus others.

The Redundancy Survival Guide, by Rebecca Corfield and Barry Cushway. ISBN 978-0749457617. This covers such issues as your legal rights in a redundancy situation, how to negotiate around different outcome options and more. It also offers good basic briefing on starting a search for a new job.

Rebuilding Your Life After Redundancy, by Janet Davies. ISBN 978-1845491017. This gives basic coverage to some of the issues and devotes much of its attention to ways to get back into work, including self-employment, volunteering, consultancy, working abroad and others.

Getting clear with money

When you are at the stage of understanding and clearing negative beliefs around money, Peter Koenig's work is very helpful. There is helpful information and useful tools on his blog (www.peterkoenig.typepad.com). His book, *30 Lies About Money: Liberating Your Life, Liberating Your Money*, ISBN 978-0-595-29236-4, is a short and powerful exposure of some of the commonest misleading beliefs about money.

At the practical level, eg looking at pensions, care costs etc, there are a number of useful UK websites. You could try the following: www.saga.co.uk, www.giddylimits.co.uk and www.mabels.org.uk.

In looking for professional help with savings, pensions and investments, you might try local Independent Financial Advisors (IFAs). You can get contacts for local ones at www.unbiased. co.uk. Look for an IFA with expertise in ethical investments: if you're unhappy about rampant capitalism, if your values include sustainability and fair trade, this is a way to match your actions and beliefs. You can contact these through www.ethicalinvest-ment.org.uk.

Chapter 5

Health: Tuning up and crash repairs

By Dr Max Mackay James

The rest of ageing, at least so far, isn't as bad as it might be. My body hangs together pretty well – the only time it's a bother is when I happen to catch sight of myself in the mirror, especially late at night after too much sight-clearing wine. The upsetting thing then is how in its softenings and sags the body looks simply stupid. It doesn't understand the way it once did how important a personage it's lugging around – otherwise it wouldn't dare appear in this gnarled disguise.

C. K. WILLIAMS (B 1936–), *ON BEING OLD*
(FROM THE UK POETRY SOCIETY ANNUAL LECTURE 2011)

Ageing? OK, so maybe you would prefer not to think about it! But here's the thing: your fifties, sixties and seventies are coming anyway. And here's another thing: if it's unmentionable, it's unmanageable. So let's talk about it, and let's play and even joke about it a little: as American poet C. K. Williams (in his mid-seventies) said with a grin and a twinkle in his eye '...Ageing, at least so far, isn't as bad as it might be'. How good could your ageing be? The first section of this chapter is about healthy lifestyles to increase your chances of enjoying good health and having less illness as you grow older. It also explores how to get motivated and succeed in making these positive changes in your life.

Case history 1

I met Ken as a mid-fifties patient in the integrated health clinic ('integrated' meant combining conventional and alternative medicine) I used to work in when I was a GP. Most of the patients we saw in the clinic had long-term illnesses, or chronic disease, as it is called by doctors. Ken was a mess: massively overweight, two previous heart attacks, serious joint problems and now cancer – fortunately a slow one and not life-threatening, but anxiety added to his other problems, and he was depressed at times too. So we had a lot to talk about during the first forty-minute session, and frankly I was feeling overwhelmed by all Ken's problems. Put together it felt hopeless. 'What do you want?' I asked near the end. 'Oh, I know I am not going to get better,' he said, 'but I wondered if you could help with…' – and Ken reeled off a precise list of six things he wanted help with: 20% more mobility, 10% less weight, 30% less joint pain, somebody to talk to about his tendency to worry and advice getting off the drug cocktail he was on. '…And the tinnitus,' Ken concluded, 'not a cure, but 20% better for the ringing in my ears please'. Ken knew exactly what he wanted, and we were able to agree a plan to give it to him.

What do you want as you get older? The second section of the chapter is about pointing you towards the best health information sources so you can be in control of your health decisions and get the best out of your health services. The focus is on online health information – where to find out about symptoms, health problems, illnesses and treatments, and the dos and don'ts of using these resources. I don't deal with specific illnesses, as the information sources I am pointing you towards will do this for you. However, it's worth mentioning that emotional and psychological health is dealt with in Chapter 7, and sexual health in Chapter 10. The holistic approach of the book means there is also overlap with other chapters as regards health issues, and these will be pointed out as you read through this chapter and elsewhere.

Case history 2

Mr A (we never used first names) came to the integrated health clinic when he was in his seventies with severe long-term leg damage from an old accident. Mr A was old-school working class and hard as nails: despite being in constant pain he didn't believe in taking pills and he didn't like wasting time talking about it. Then a year later he got seriously ill with an aggressive kind of cancer. He knew he was going to die, but he remained a fighter, and, still refusing painkillers, he soldiered on – alone – to the despair of his wife and family. I respected his way, but I couldn't help wondering how different it could have been if he had been able to open up more and ask for help.

Do you know how to ask for help? It's a challenging question at the best of times, but even more important to know the answer when you fall sick with a serious illness. We can't do it alone, and the third section of this chapter deals with navigating serious illness. It also offers practical advice on dealing with health services, and how to ask for help and support for healing and hope, and especially how to mobilise a healing team around you.

HEALTHY LIFESTYLES

Many middle-aged men tend to ignore their bodies altogether and carry on almost as if they don't exist. Fortunately, the body is the most loyal and forgiving of friends, and mostly it puts up with this neglect: but in the long run, health problems, many of which are avoidable, can develop. So the first piece of health advice is to begin getting to know and positively making friends with your body again. For instance, try looking at your near-naked body in a full-length mirror in the morning, preferably in nothing more than your underpants. Yes, I know, it can be a shock or maybe it's your body's idea of a bad joke!

Rather than dismissing the evidence, or feeling angry or even ashamed about the look of your older body, I recommend you spend a moment each day having a smile about your appearance, seeing the realities of ageing for what they are and gently sharing in your older body's way of joking. Your body and you will get on much better if you do.

Move more!

The information provided below is based on the latest UK Government Department of Health and NHS Guidelines and Recommendations (www.nhs.uk/livewell/Pages/Livewellhub. aspx).

Physical exercise: Thirty minutes a day

Here's the bottom line based on the best research evidence: you need to commit 150 minutes (two and a half hours) each week to engage in physical activity. There are no 'ifs' or 'maybes', and it's an ongoing necessity as you get older. Making this a regular habit will significantly reduce your risk of developing serious and dangerous illness, such as heart disease, diabetes, asthma, stroke and some cancers. More than that, it will also help you to lose weight: a 60kg (10 stone) person walking for thirty minutes burns 150 calories, and will help your sense of physical, mental and emotional wellbeing. Breaking the 150 minutes down, you need to do at least thirty minutes of physical activity such as 'fast walking' on five days of the week (thirty minutes every day would be even better, but it's okay to have a couple of days off each week if you have to).

What is 'fast walking'? It means going at a good pace of about 4mph. It is not strolling down to the pub or across the car park of your local supermarket, dawdling up and down the aisles, going through check-out and heading back to the car. This kind of physical activity is called 'moderate-intensity physical activity', and it means doing enough to raise your heart rate and break a sweat. You are doing enough if you're able to talk, but not sing the words to your favourite song. Fast walking and cycling are the most common types of 'moderate-intensity physical activity', but there's also jogging, dancing, swimming, badminton, tennis, etc.

Here are ways to think about including exercise into your daily routine so that it becomes a regular habit:

◆ Walk part of every journey

◆ Try fast walking to the shops

◆ Go swimming twice a week

◆ Use the stairs instead of the lift

◆ Leave the car behind for short journeys

◆ Cycle to the shops or a favourite outdoor space

◆ Do a regular walk with a friend

◆ Go for a good walk with family or friends in the evening (say one hour after dinner).

The good news is that you don't have to do this physical activity all in one chunk. You can break it up into blocks of ten to fifteen minutes. It's also important to avoid sitting in one place for too long, for instance in front of a computer screen or the television. Look at your watch when you first sit down and take regular breaks every forty minutes if you're going to be sitting or working in one place.

The basic recommendation for 150 minutes of moderate-intensity physical activity each week doesn't change or get less as men get older. You need to keep being active into your sixties, seventies and eighties to keep the risk of chronic illness down.

If you're not used to physical activity, building up to a session of thirty-minute fast walking will take some time. Increase exercise levels gradually. If you can only walk fast for a couple of minutes to begin with, that's fine. Don't overdo it on the first few days and don't injure yourself by being overambitious. You can also break up your activity into ten-minute chunks, so long as you are doing it at a moderate intensity. Listen to how your body is feeling – it's a trustworthy guide: if it's complaining, slow down. Don't be in too much hurry to succeed, do a little more every day and slowly increase your exercise time over the weeks.

If you have any concerns or worries about how your body feels when you exercise, go to your GP.

If you're overweight or obese and aiming to lose weight as well as get fitter, you should increase physical activity to around sixty to ninety minutes on at least five days of the week (a total of between 300 and 450 minutes per week). To lose weight, you not only need to exercise more than 150 minutes a week, but also make changes to your diet (See the Lose Weight! section below).

Want to move even more? Go to www.menbeyond50.net for more healthy lifestyle resources (Goldmine and Toolkit 'Body and Mind' sections):

a) Organisations to help you engage in a wide variety of physical activities in the UK.

b) Advice on Vigorous Intensity Exercise and muscle strengthening.

c) Longer walking and bicycling programmes, and getting involved in 'Green Gym' projects.

Eat well!

Over the millennia human beings have become adapted to eating an incredibly broad and diverse range of foods, but modern eating habits (both undereating and overeating, and eating too much of the 'wrong' kinds of food) have now created a huge number of health problems and illnesses, of which the biggest problem today is, of course, obesity. There's also increasing research evidence that having a bad diet significantly increases your risks of developing serious illness, such as heart disease, stroke, gut (gastro-intestinal) disorders and disease, diabetes and some cancers, especially bowel-related cancers. Food and diet are very complex territories, so I'm going to stick to the absolute basic advice for which the research evidence is the strongest.

Five servings of fruit and vegetables each day

The core message is that you need to eat at least five portions of a variety of fruit and vegetables per day (a portion weighs 80g). That's five portions of fruit and veg altogether, not five portions of each. These should be eaten in place of foods which are higher in fat and calories. For example, if you feel hungry between meals, dried or fresh fruit makes a good healthy snack, rather than chocolate or a sweet biscuit. I'm sure you are getting the picture!

Important general advice about healthy eating is to eat three meals a day, always have breakfast and don't skip meals. Skipping meals will just make you feel more hungry, think more about food and more likely to overeat in the evening or snack between meals. The best part about this 'five-a-day' approach is that it's potentially both enjoyable and delicious! Initially you may find it strange to get used to, and there are many sources of help and support, both on where to find interesting recipes and how to cook healthy meals this way.

Go to www.menbeyond50.net for more healthy lifestyle resources (Goldmine and Toolkit 'Body and Mind' sections):

a) What foods count towards five-a-day eating.

b) Healthy eating five-a-day cooking ideas.

Lose weight!

It's official: obesity is a world epidemic, and many people are seriously overweight. If you're surprised looking at your near-naked body and the bulges showing around your middle in the mirror, you may already have a sneaky feeling that you are one of them.

The serious health risks of being overweight are the same as for being inactive and having a poor diet, but this time disabling and painful long-term physical problems and illnesses such as arthritis, joint problems and especially bad backs are added to the list of dangers.

So maybe you think you might need to lose weight, but here's the challenge – do you actually want to? Motivation is absolutely key, and it's important to take the time to explore and develop your personal reasons for wanting to lose weight. Perhaps you want to change the way you look or feel about yourself. Losing weight can make you feel more energetic and self-confident. Be honest about this. Identify what drives you and make sure you're setting your own goals, not doing it for other people.

Losing weight also requires a systematic plan. Do not do 'crash diets': the research shows that except in the very short term, they don't work. A well-planned six-week programme to lose weight has far more chance of succeeding than a few days of starvation. I sometimes think it's like getting one of those complicated 'flat-pack' (sorry, bad pun!) furniture packs for home assembly. You know that to get it right you need to give it time, have lots of patience, be systematic in your approach and not cut any corners. Use the same approach for losing weight.

Your plan will have much more chance of success if it involves other people. For some, this will be through the encouragement, support and backup of a partner or special friend. Others may prefer to be in a bigger formal or informal group, and there are many different dieting organisations to choose from. Many of these will have more women than men in them, but it is also possible to find men-only dieting groups. I am not going to recommend any particular organisations as there are very many of them and they are easy to find through the internet.

Go to the end of the chapter for a 'Motivation checklist', and go to www.menbeyond50.net for a six-week weight reduction programme (Goldmine and Toolkit 'Body and Mind' sections).

Healthy lifestyle motivation checklist

◆ Always take the time to clarify your motivation. Decide what it is you want to achieve in advance, always be honest with yourself and be prepared to modify your aims if necessary as you proceed. Set off on the right course with the right intentions and you'll have the best chance of achieving your aims.

◆ Set realistic goals. Avoid high expectations that will leave you disappointed. As part of a longer, steady journey, you are far more likely to succeed by taking small steps one at a time.

◆ Exercise your imagination as well as your body. For instance, take time to visualise yourself losing weight, exercising or eating healthier meals. Imagining positive outcomes and mentally rehearsing can really help you succeed in the actual practice.

◆ Make good habits. Create routines for yourself and get a bit obsessional about 'same time, same place' commitments.

◆ Use your mind as your personal trainer. Find different ways of sharpening your mental focus and also of relaxing the mind – this can really help you create a healthier lifestyle. The practice of mindfulness is a good approach (try www.getsomeheadspace.com).

◆ Don't put off the start day. Watch out for any unhelpful mental habits you may have, or negative or critical voices in your head that tell you, 'You are never going to get started', or make excuses for not doing it. Treat the chatter kindly but firmly and simply let the negative stuff all go as passing thoughts.

◆ Learn to be flexible. It is inevitable that you are going to miss the occasional targets or sessions week by week. Don't beat yourself up about missing a day or two of exercise, or eating the wrong foods, but simply make sure you get back to your routine the next day.

◆ Make sure you enjoy yourself. A healthy lifestyle can be fun, and it doesn't have to be a grind or feel like a chore. Identify the bits you like and enjoy, note the feel-good moments when they arise and do more of the things that produce them.

◆ Congratulate yourself regularly on the journey. Whether it's exercising or losing weight, use your achievements for positive reinforcement.

◆ Integrate body, mind and spirit. See a healthy lifestyle as part and parcel of your whole new way of life and not as something outside. Be on the lookout for ways to integrate the healthy lifestyle into other aspects of your life and you will become altogether happier and feel more fulfilled, as well as healthier.

SEARCHING FOR HEALTH INFORMATION

Helping you to plan and stay in control as you make important health decisions, whether it's looking for lifestyle advice, information on a serious illness, or finding out about a specific health problem, symptoms or treatments, there are many high-quality and free sources of trustworthy health information. However, be warned, the world is also filled with fools, sirens and health charlatans, who peddle fictitious treatments, promise impossible cures and many of whom provide dangerous advice. This can sometimes make the shipwreck of a serious illness much worse, and even damage your health.

Online health 'gateway sites'

I am strongly in favour of using the internet to find health information, and my advice is always to use online health 'gateway sites' as your primary ports of call. Rather than putting the symptoms or illness name directly into a general Google search, always go to one of these gateway sites first and then do your first searches from there.

The Health on the Net Foundation (www.hon.ch) provides a HON Code Certification for health information medical websites and it is a useful kitemark to look out for when searching:

 Good gateway sites will always display this sign.

In the UK, the NHS provides an enormous amount of online information sources. However, the oceans of NHS information are so vast it's not always easy to find what you're looking for. Depending on the general area you are searching, there are three different NHS sites you need to know about:

- ◆ *NHS Choices* (www.nhs.uk/conditions/Pages/hub.aspx): for information on illness and diseases, dealing with over 800 conditions, including all the major serious illnesses.

- ◆ *NHS Direct* (www.nhsdirect.nhs.uk): for health advice dealing mainly with everyday symptoms, and advising where to go for treatment.

- ◆ *NHS Live Well* (www.nhs.uk/LiveWell/Pages/Livewellhub. aspx): for healthy lifestyle information and advice (high-quality and research-based).

A number of registered charities are also health gateway sites. My top choices are www.patient.co.uk and www.malehealth. co.uk (run by the Male Health Forum www.menshealthfo-rum.org.uk). Both these sites do everything good gateway sites should; the advice is kept up to date, it's simple to find your way around the site and undertake searches, and the jargon-free information is easy to understand.

On any of these health gateway sites type the name of your illness or health problem into their search box, or the particular symptom or name of the disease if you already know it. This will take you to the specific area about which you are looking for information. A good idea is to use two health gateway sites and compare the results, say both Patient.co.uk and NHS Choices. Go to the www.menbeyond50.net website for more recommended online health information resources (Goldmine and Toolkit 'Body and Mind' sections).

Advice about alternative medicine

Finding information about alternative medicine can be both confusing and problematic. My advice is to use RCCM, Research

Council for Complementary Medicine (www.rccm.org.uk). Note this site is HON Code Certified, while nearly all other complementary and alternative medicine sites are not. I'm not saying that some of these other sites aren't worth looking at, but I suggest your first port of call is the RCCM. It also has a useful index which explains the various alternative medicine approaches, with links to all their main organisations. These will explain in greater detail about the particular treatment methods and will usually list practitioners in your area. I suggest you telephone a few of these in order to assess their professional approach (and their level of charges), before making a first appointment. Word-of-mouth recommendation can sometimes also work as an additional way of finding a practitioner, but always try to find two or three opinions before finally deciding.

NAVIGATING SERIOUS ILLNESS

Even as you are hopefully living some of your best and most creative years in your fifties, sixties and beyond, at a certain point a serious illness may strike, or there may be a severe worsening of the symptoms of a longer-term illness, tipping the balance.

When you fall seriously ill, what you want are treatments that are safe and effective to get you better in the shortest possible time. You need to have confidence that the medicine you are going to take actually works. Good medicine is also about trusting the healing environment in which the treatment is being given, including your relationships with all the people involved and the way the medical service is being provided.

I like to think of the search to find good medicine as a sea voyage across both charted and uncharted oceans with you as the skipper. What follows below is a guide for crossing these vast and sometimes stormy waters of serious illness, to help you successfully navigate your way. There are two elements to being a good skipper. Firstly, you need to know how to read the stars and chart your way, and where to find reliable and trustworthy health information to help you make your health decisions (see the major section above for more on this). Secondly, you need the seamanship skills to control your craft and continue to steer your way in a storm, and to know how to look after yourself during a serious illness.

The shock of a major illness

Some illnesses like arthritis progress slowly, and there will be a gradual worsening of symptoms over time, but many illnesses come on without any warning. This is especially true of life-threatening illnesses such as heart attacks or strokes, and some cancers. It's helpful to understand that although you age gradually through life, decline in health through serious illness often happens suddenly.

This sudden change to your whole life through the onset of a serious illness is an enormous shock. Losing your health is possibly the worst shipwreck most people suffer in life, but it's not the end of your life. If you're physically changed by a serious illness you will find yourself going through a grieving process over how your body used to be and the health you have lost, but it's not the end, you do keep on going. For more about handling the grieving and emotional effects of a serious illness and major loss of health, go to Chapter 2.

The challenge of a life-threatening illness can also be a potential awakening, both to what you are leaving behind and to what's potentially available to you through healing and renewal. In fact, being faced with the reality of your own possible death is the biggest life-affirming opportunity for making your big choices and decisions.

Bad news sucks!

Nobody likes getting bad news, and being told you have a dangerous life-threatening illness is about as bad as it gets. Research shows that how you get on in the early days of becoming seriously ill depends a lot on how the bad news was first given to you. This depends both on how the doctors and nurses break the news to you and to your partner and family, as well as the way you react, and how well you can take the news in to begin with. Good or bad first experiences impact powerfully on how well or badly you get on through your illness, and you do need to be aware that some doctors and nurses are good at breaking bad news, and others are not. This is not a particular criticism of the medical profession. None of us likes giving bad news and it's always difficult to do.

So you need to know how these first 'bad news' conversations typically go so you can prepare in advance. Consultations or appointments at hospitals with doctors or nurses are usually where the bad news about a serious illness is first given. If you have not been feeling well for some time and suspect you may have a serious illness, you're likely to be worried already. You may not have been sleeping well, and feeling anxious and frightened is not the best state of mind to receive information, especially bad news.

Planning and organising your health resources

From the time when you first receive the bad news to finding healing and hope, and the time of your eventual recovery, here are three important guidelines:

1. *Manage your meetings with doctors positively* (and with nurses and other healthcare professionals).

Plan ahead and make sure you always ask your most important questions! It's easy to forget this in the stress and worry of an appointment. My advice for all consultations with healthcare professionals is to write down the questions which you most want answered. Do this in advance of your first appointment and before subsequent visits too. Don't make the list too long. Two or three questions each visit are usually about as much as you can cope with in the time and under the stress of your appointment. Examples of questions about your illness include:

◆ What is the name of my illness?

◆ Is there a diagnosis?

- What is the best treatment?

- Are there other treatment options?

- How do I find out more about my illness?

2. *Organise yourself in advance*

Like planning a trip abroad, in advance of a medical procedure, especially if it involves staying in hospital, get organised as much as you can. When you travel you have to think of all the things you need to take with you, and it's the same with a serious illness.

You especially need to think ahead and prepare if you're going to hospital and your stay there is going to be more than a few days. Getting out as soon as possible is of course the main purpose of your planning. (No disrespect to nurses and doctors, but hospitals are rarely pleasant places to stay.)

3. *Find a health advocate: Make your illness a 'we' experience*

The best journeys are generally those made in the company of somebody else and not alone, and the same is true of the potentially long and arduous journey of a major illness. Making your illness a 'we' relationship with somebody else can transform the experience, provide you with hope when you're feeling down and help you mobilise all your healing resources. In fact, having a companion with you who is prepared to accompany you through thick and thin, who can also speak up for you when you cannot find the words yourself, is probably the single most beneficial thing you can do to help yourself when you are ill.

Be bold when asking somebody for help! From the outset of your illness, try to find somebody close to you who you trust, and you think is prepared to go with you to all your appointments and consultations with healthcare professionals. If you want to talk about the situation with your chosen companion before the appointment, and what you are expecting to happen, this can be a good idea too. If you have written down your most important questions, you can perhaps ask them to write down the answers for you, as best they understand them, during the appointment. Tell them to write down anything else the doctors or nurses are saying if you think it is important, and give them permission to ask for more explanation if something does not make sense to them.

These trusted health companions in the 'we' relationship are often called 'health advocates'. A health advocate may be your partner, a family member or close friend, but they may be somebody else who you don't know so well, but is able and prepared to take on the role. They can be adults, sons or daughters (if over sixteen), siblings or parents, as well as friends and even, perhaps, professionals. If you want to ask somebody to be your advocate, trust your intuition and simply go ahead and ask. The prime role of an advocate is to support you. Much of this is practical:

◆ Putting out the call for help among your family and friends and coordinating offers.

◆ Taking care of the home front and making sure family needs are not forgotten.

◆ Speaking with healthcare professionals when you want.

◆ Writing down your medical history as it progresses.

◆ Helping to plan and organise everything.

◆ Keeping your notebook of names, dates and places up to date.

◆ Setting goals and rewards on your road to recovery.

A health advocate will also provide healing and hope. This doesn't require special skills, it's simply about them retaining their humanity at all times, being relentlessly upbeat and having a great sense of humour. These qualities will help you cultivate yours and lift your mood. Having humanity also means that there is no such thing as giving up in their vocabulary. Health advocates can give you courage and won't run away from the challenges, even when you are feeling like doing so. Above all they will always put your wishes first.

The above may appear idealistic, but as a doctor I have seen many people in the 'we' relationships of patient and advocate, and observed what a major difference it has made to the experience of a serious illness and the long-term outcomes. Even when it is 'bad news' I have felt inspired by the ability of patients and advocates to keep going together, pushing the possibilities for healing and hope, care and recovery, and maintaining an open-hearted spirit in every situation, however challenging.

Patient support and self-help groups can also help. Use the Patient.co.uk self-help page which has links to 1,852 groups listed in the UK currently (www.patient.co.uk/selfhelp.asp), and also their Health Advocacy page for information on helpful organisations (www.patient.co.uk/directory/patient-advocacy-advice). In addition, the UK charity Healthtalkonline (www.healthtalkonline.org) provides a major resource where you can listen online to well-researched factual accounts and patient stories.

Go to www.menbeyond50.net for more navigating serious illness resources (Goldmine and Toolkit 'Body and Mind' sections):

a) Practical checklist for questions to ask your doctor or healthcare professional.

b) Practical checklist for being organised in hospital.

c) Practical checklist for health advocacy.

d) Healing practice exercises.

A pathway through illness

Serious illness is an up-and-down rollercoaster! Sometimes in the eye of the storm all you can feel is terror and panic. At other times it's possible to begin looking ahead and even discover the positive 'wake-up call' aspects of a life-threatening illness. In my opinion it's not about coping or not coping. Sometimes, even if you're not getting better from a serious illness or there's a relapse, you can have the feeling that you are successfully engaging with the sickness and are recovering control of your life. Other times you can feel so threatened and overwhelmed by the illness, even during a period of recuperation, that you feel you're going crazy and are being thrown into a deep pit of despair. Remember, too, that illness is not all tragedy and some parts of it can be darkly funny. Let go into those funny moments, and whenever you can, find the comic side to your situation and have a good laugh (laughter is the best medicine!).

There's no right or wrong way to go through the storms of a major life-threatening sickness. The experience changes on a daily or even on an hourly basis, and doesn't necessarily fit into the neat and orderly life narrative of what was the previously secure 'me' before you fell ill. The boundaries between our sense of self, our physical bodies and the living world are not as certain as we might like to think, and powerful energies and healing can manifest even during the darkest moments of the journey.

A pathway through illness? Yes, if we are open to seeing the possibilities of healing and hope, and living every day, however challenging, to the full!

RESOURCES

I don't know of a one-stop superhealth/superhealing book, but the following list is a mix of my favourites, and some of the better health information and self-help books:

A Bloke's Diagnose-It-Yourself Guide to Health, by Dr Keith Hopcroft and Dr Alistair Moulds (2000). ISBN 978-0192628251. An A–Z of common complaints and health problems and what to do about them.

The Power of Two: Surviving Serious Illness with an Attitude and an Advocate, by Brian Monaghan and Gerri Monaghan. ISBN 978-0761152590. An inspiring and practical 'experience and common sense' book by a husband and wife team in a strong 'we' relationship (he has cancer, she is his health advocate).

Anticancer: A New Way of Life, by David Servan-Schreiber. ISBN 978-0718156848. A 'positive guide' by a doctor from the holistic perspective, and at the same time a journey though illness from the inside and towards a future death (David Servan-Schreiber has now died from his cancer).

Preventing and Surviving Heart Attacks, by Dr Tom Smith. ISBN 978-8122202670. A 'positive guide book' for this important topic.

Healing Without Freud and Prozac, by David Servan-Schreiber. ISBN 978-1447211464. A natural and holistic approach to curing stress, anxiety and depression.

Healing into Life and Death, by Stephen Levine. ISBN 978-0946551484. A practice-orientated book for finding healing, and exploring the many ways to engage with the challenges of serious illness and a future death.

The Warmth of the Heart Prevents your Body from Rusting, by Marie de Hennezel. ISBN 978-1905744848. A compassionate exploration by a French doctor of the perils and pleasures of ageing.

Middle Age: A Natural History, by David Bainbridge. ISBN 978-1846272677. Explores the science (it's written by a vet) and how best to respond to the physical and natural phenomena of ageing.

Finding Meaning in the Second Half of Life, by James Hollis. ISBN 978-1592402076. A Jungian psychotherapist explores the natural phenomena of ageing from the psychological perspective.

Chapter 6

Family dynamics:
Ageing parents and lots more

'Why keep in touch with them? That's what I want to know,' asked Larry despairingly. 'What satisfaction does it give you? They're all either fossilized or mental.'

GERALD DURRELL, *MY FAMILY AND OTHER ANIMALS*

For many men beyond fifty, the family is one of the more immoveable and baffling parts of their life. After all, you can't divorce your parents or retire from being father to your kids. Bust-ups within a family can be some of the most bitter and hard to resolve. And on the other hand, family life can be a great source of sweetness in your maturing years. This chapter explores some of the main changes and issues you are likely to face in this life stage: our journey starts with ageing parents, moves on through grown-up kids, and completes with brothers and sisters.

Have you ever thought about the character or flavour of your extended family as a whole? If they were a movie, what would it be? *Gone with the Wind*? *Four Weddings and a Funeral*? *Who's Afraid of Virginia Woolf*?? *The Flintstones*? If you remember the idea from Chapter 2 that you may repeat the same dramas and stories in your life, see if that's true for your family. It amazes me how often I see patterns repeating in a family, such as the role of the eldest child, conflicts, infidelity and addictions.

As George Bernard Shaw said, 'If you cannot get rid of the family skeleton, you may as well make it dance'. If you can gently start to name the patterns you see and spread that awareness through even part of the family, things may start to change. Bringing humour and visibility to family dynamics can be very healing. The favourite game at gatherings of my family is Therapy (a board game from Milton Bradley), in which players rate themselves and each other on questions like how judgemental/patient/dreamy they are.

AGEING PARENTS

It could happen sooner, but for many men it's somewhere beyond fifty that they meet a watershed point, where their parents become dependent and fragile, and leadership in the family passes to the next generation. This change may happen in smooth ways or bumpy ones, but it's often a big emotional challenge for you as a maturing man. Suddenly you feel older, closer to death, like you are carrying more responsibilities.

Many years ago, when my father was in his healthy early seventies, I was phoned out of the blue from Massachusetts by Steve, an American friend. I almost never get calls from the US so the fact he phoned was a big deal. Steve's father had died completely unexpectedly of a heart attack in his late sixties. Steve simply said to me, 'I'm calling to urge you to say whatever you need to say to your father before he dies, now. However healthy he is, don't wait.'

I followed Steve's advice, and the conversation I had with my father led to a much more open and deep relationship between us for the fifteen years until he died at 89. So just imagine, if your father or mother was dying today, what would you want to say now? Most parents judge themselves harshly, so it could be very healing for them to hear you say that you know they did their best, that you thank them for all the good things they gave you, that you forgive them and that you love them.

You may have spent a lot of your childhood and adult life feeling angry towards your parents, as I did, but you're all losing out if you remain stuck with this. For me, losing my marriage at forty-nine, and seeing how my parents supported me and my kids, woke me up. I finally realised that the parents I was angry with were young, naive and long gone. When I looked at my parents now, I saw two good-hearted, loving people who still had their blind spots, but were giving me a lot of support, despite my own shortcomings. When I finally chose to forgive them, it enriched all our lives. If you're finding this hard to do, think what you'd like as a parent from your kids, whether or not you actually have any. Surely you need understanding and forgiveness, and so do your parents.

As your parents get older, they may become more cranky, irritable and set in their ways. They may find it humiliating to have their hearing, mobility or other faculties deteriorate. It may be hard for them to move from being a dependable parent to a dependent one. These changes may be upsetting for you too. When my father had a stroke at eighty-four, he soon could not walk without help. He had always taken care of his appearance, and now he looked unkempt.

For several months I found the changes so upsetting that it was hard to be with him. Then I realised that my distress came from my own fear of being infirm and dependent like him. In fact, my father was handling the changes with courage. At last I got beyond my own feelings and began to consider what he might need from me. When I could relate to him as a person, find ways to enjoy being together, value all the good qualities he still had, celebrate his courage and avoid seeming to pity him, our relationship flourished in a new way. The changes and crises you may face with your parents could be quite different in detail, but these principles should help you too.

Home care and care homes

Having been involved with many men's groups over a long time I've seen a lot of maturing men help their parents face these issues. It can be a painful time, not only for the parents, but for you as a son, and it can cause serious disputes between family members.

You may have two parents still together, two separated, or just one surviving: at some stage, issues of care will probably arise. Maybe your parents are still in the family home and it's getting too much for them. Often one parent is infirm and the other is being dragged down by providing all the care. Or one parent has died, and the other is bewildered and overwhelmed by life. At some stage as your parents age, it will help you all if you can start talking honestly about issues like care, dying, funerals and wills, as well as feelings.

This kind of honesty is rare in British families, and your parents may be too upset and even embarrassed by their situation to initiate it. If such openness is unusual in your family, move towards it gently, choosing a minor issue to start with, accepting that you may be met with anger or silence at first. Realise that the embarrassment you feel may be yours, not your parents'. For example, I was upset the first time I discussed care provision for my parents with them, but they had been thinking about it for months and were relieved to speak about it with me.

The practical issues around who provides care, residential care homes and finances are hugely complex, so see Resources for more help on this. An important general principle is to separate the facts from the emotion and prejudice which you, your parents and the rest of the family may feel. The strong feelings are understandable and you need to acknowledge them, but don't base your decisions on them. When my father had his stroke, my mother cared for him at home on her own for a year, but it was clear that her health was starting to suffer. Most of our family, including me, felt that putting a parent in a care home was a heartless act, a disgrace to the family, a bit like sending a relative to the workhouse in Dickensian times.

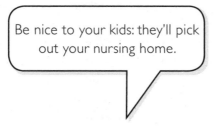

Be nice to your kids: they'll pick out your nursing home.

In practice, when my mother, brother and I visited a few care homes locally, we found some that felt genuinely caring and congenial. Understandably, my father was upset at the prospect of leaving the family house and 'being put in a home', and was already too fragile to listen to reason. Several of us had conversations hearing his feelings, and gently explaining that if we did not take this step, his wife's health would suffer seriously. This is a situation where you need a strong consensus within the family, and also have to accept that the parent going into residential care may not fully understand and accept the move.

Thankfully, once he was in a care home, my father accepted the situation pretty well. In a strange way, he was quite happy there, and I've seen this with others: a good care home is a safe and supportive place, especially when you know that you are fragile and vulnerable. It has a reality of its own, and the rest of the family have to judge carefully how much of the outside world to bring in. For example, after a few months I thought it would be a treat to give my father an outing and take him back to the family home. In fact, he found it disorienting and upsetting to be back in a reality that had now disappeared for him.

If you have one parent living in residential care and the other at home, it could be the parent at home who needs most support. They may feel guilty about sending their partner away, and even if there were strains in the relationship, they're probably feeling lonely. You can't magic these things away, but you can increase your contact with them. If you can also encourage your children and their grandparents to be in touch more, it can be very sweet for everyone.

My experience of care homes is that the relatives need to keep an eye on how things are working, and it helps if one or two of the family have regular contact with the manager. Your parent may be complaining: perhaps validly, but perhaps because they're anxious generally or want more of your attention. Care homes often have high staff turnover, and new carers might not understand what your parent needs. You may reach stages where you have to move your parent from one care home to another. This might arise because the current place cannot provide the level of support needed or you feel unhappy with the quality of care. These decisions need careful explanation and negotiation within the family and with the parent involved.

One feature of life for many people in care homes is that much of their attention is focused on very local issues, like the food, staff or the other residents. This may be sad for you, but ask yourself if it's okay for your parent. Will it help them if you talk about the outside world? I remember a rare time when I found my father depressed, because he was feeling useless. I pointed out how much he could bring to the people around him by appreciating them. And I suggested that as he sat in his room, he might pray for each of his friends and family. He told me later how much those ideas had helped him.

Finance is a hard thing to discuss in most families, but you'll need to talk about it if residential care comes up. The typical annual cost of a residential care home in 2012 was around £26,000. If your parents can release capital by selling their home, this may have to be faced. But you and your brothers or sisters may also have to discuss your possible role in funding residential care.

It may be easier for your parents to have a carer visit them or even live in their existing home. This also needs careful separation of emotion and practicalities. Home care needs more managing by someone, and the rest of the family will probably need to step in at times, for example with holiday cover. All this can deepen the links within the family, but it can also stress them.

Have you made a will yet?

Not an easy conversation starter, is it? But as you try to create a climate of honesty for both facts and feelings around ageing and dying, you need to talk about wills. For a start, you may be named as an executor, perhaps along with brothers or sisters. Your parents may be uneasy about disclosing details of bequests and finances, and you should respect that. But you need to know where their will, bank details and legal documents are kept, and if they have a solicitor who can help sort out the estate. You may be reluctant to raise this subject, but if your parent dies without a will, the hassle will probably fall on your shoulders and there'll be a lot more of it. If your parent needs help in drafting a will, see Resources.

When a parent dies

In some ways you can prepare yourself for a parent's death, and in some ways the actual impact can't be anticipated. In the years before my father died, I talked to several maturing men about their feelings after a parent's death: it helped me understand how I might feel, and made me realise the qualities I wanted in my relationship with my dad before he went. It also seems to help bereaved men to be able to talk like this with another man.

Other ways you can prepare are to say the things you need to (see above) and to talk openly about the practicalities: not only the will, but also about what kind of funeral, burial or cremation, who should be invited to the funeral and how to find their contact details. It can be helpful for you and your parent to discuss how they feel about dying and what they believe happens after death. In grieving my father, it uplifted me to know that he was calm about dying and positive about what lay beyond.

When a parent dies, brace yourself for a couple of extraordinary weeks. If you can make some space for your own grieving, then do: but you're likely to find your time fully taken up with practicalities and other people. The funeral has to be organised and invitations sent out. A lot of time goes in relatives and friends simply wanting to talk to you, share their feelings and be heard.

Funerals have many forms and moods. You may not have much influence on this: the parent may have prescribed what they wanted and you have the rest of the family to negotiate with. If there's a chance for you to speak your personal truth about your parent at their funeral, take it: for me, my father's funeral was a real rite of passage, a big experience in finding my voice in a time of loss, and sharing my feelings in a family that can be too restrained.

My advice about bereavement is that it's best to make time *after* the funeral to open up to your own feelings and then consider how your life moves forward from here. Take a few days off and rest. The strength of feelings around a death and funeral can be exhausting. The passing of a parent is a life-changing experience, but nobody can foretell in what way for you. It may confront you with your own mortality and the sense that your generation is now the next to go, so this might be a call to face your own feelings about dying.

I found that the feelings of loss, sadness and confusion after my father died came back in waves: there was no way of predicting when they would happen, but I made time to go into the emotions whenever I could. Marking the anniversary of a parent's death can be a good way of reconnecting with them, seeing what their life means to you now, and celebrating them, hopefully with other members of your family.

For much more detailed guides to both the emotional and practical aspects of losing a parent, see the books in Resources.

WHEN YOUR KIDS BECOME ADULTS

How has your relationship with your children evolved as they move through the teenage years and into adulthood? How do you imagine it in the years ahead? Often these relationships don't evolve gradually, but in fits and starts through major events: leaving school, a new home, a wedding, and sometimes through major arguments as well. Modern times are tough ones for any young adult to find a steady sense of self and earn a good living: so you may find that your kids are under stress and uncertainty at the same time as you are.

> **'There are three ways to get something done: do it yourself, employ someone or forbid your children to do it.'**
> *Mona Crane*

Your relationship with your children may have all kinds of flavours during your maturing years. They may resent you for growing up in easier times and for having more wealth than they do. They may expect you to make things right still and bail them out. Or you may find that the friendship between you deepens and that you help each other. This can be quite an edgy time between you and your kids, and it's a period when your relationship with them probably needs to be reinvented several times over.

Be honest about what's going on for you in your life generally, and if something feels awkward between you and your kids, name it and try to discuss it with them openly. Secondly, treat them more like adults, meaning that you and they have your own views and your own needs, and some balance needs to be found between them. You don't have to do everything for them and sacrifice yourself, but nor can you expect that they'll be completely independent of you. This section highlights some of the typical issues you may face.

◆ *Money.* Many men over fifty will be in a better financial position than their kids, although their future earning potential is better than yours. Your kids may ask you to fund the deposit on a house or help pay off student loans. You have to judge what's fair and if you want to set terms for any money you provide. It doesn't have to be a gift: you could make it a loan or even a joint venture; if you have funded a 20% deposit to help your son or daughter buy a flat, you could ask for 20% of the proceeds when it's eventually sold. These discussions can be tricky, because your kids have grown up looking to you to provide money and other resources, and they may not *want* to be treated as full-grown adults. Beware of kids trying to guilt-trip you into funding them. If in doubt, ask a couple of friends for a sanity check.

◆ *Fairness.* Do you remember when your kids were young how important it was to be fair and even-handed in what you gave them? For many kids, this remains a highly emotive issue, even when they're grown-up. You have to make a point of seeing these things from the viewpoint of your kids, not judging by your own standards. The fact that one of your adult children may have less money than another may not justify different treatment in their eyes. A friend of mine had three adult kids, one on low income, two high earners. He wanted to give the low earner the deposit to buy a flat, but realised he should offer a similar amount to the other two, even though they didn't need it in a practical sense. You might not want to go this far, but you have to assume that inequalities will be noticed and can upset someone. As a minimum, be upfront and discuss it with all your kids before you commit to something.

◆ *Housing.* It may be great to have an adult kid still living with you, but for how long and on what terms? Is it fair to charge them rent? You may find yourself in edgy country, where you and your offspring have different views about what's a fair arrangement. The term *boomerang kids* has been coined to describe adult children who keep coming back to live with their parents. It's important for you to keep a sense of what feels fair and acceptable to you, and find a way to be both honest and gentle with your son or daughter.

◆ *Advice.* This has been one of the most delicate areas for me since my girls turned adult. Sometimes they really want a guiding opinion, sometimes they just want supportive agreement, irrespective of what you actually think on the issue. How to know what's really needed can be tricky. Even if I have a strong view, I put it cautiously.

◆ *Crises.* It's only natural that the crises of your adult kids will affect you and probably involve you. They may have trouble finding a job or a career. It may be more serious: depression, drugs and other ways of going off the rails. Your own feelings about the crisis may be aggravated by a sense that you've helped cause it, through the way you brought your kids up. However, it won't help your kids to face their problems if **you** take responsibility for them. Set your own feelings about the past aside, focus on supporting your son or daughter right now and help them take responsibility for their situation. They may want your advice, but avoid telling them what to do since that risks disempowering them.

◆ *Dates, partners, spouses – theirs.* In your maturing years, your kids' relationships may go through ups and downs, but will hopefully settle into something happy and stable. You may feel a loss as your offspring find their main relationship outside the original family: it's part of the shift to a more adult–adult connection, so try to embrace the new shape of things. The classic stress point is when you find your son or daughter's partner difficult or feel they are unsuitable. This is one case where honesty probably won't help. You'll fare better if you can support and accept them both as fully as you can. Maybe you're missing the bigger role you had as a dad when your kids were growing up, and you must meet that need some other way.

◆ *Dates, partners, spouses – yours.* If you're no longer with the mother of your children, connecting the kids with your new amour(s) is often tricky. For a few years after my marriage ended, my daughters wanted no knowledge of my love life, let alone contact with Dad's girlfriends. There came a time when I decided to push them gently: this was when I'd been in a steady relationship for two years! It's only human to want your kids to approve of your new partner, and pretty natural for them to be guarded. Over time, if they see you're really happy in this relationship, they're likely to open up to it.

◆ *Grandchildren.* Dynamics in the whole family change when your children have children, and mostly for the better. Maturing men often find that their relationship with their son or daughter becomes more adult to adult, more easy. Part of the change is that your own kids are now creating a family with its own values and culture. These may differ from the family you created as a dad. You might need to be careful to avoid passing on your own values and beliefs too strongly to your grandchildren: it could cause friction between you and the parents.

BROTHERS AND SISTERS

I hate my brother. The only reason I speak to him is because you never know when you might need a kidney.

LILY SAVAGE

Tensions with adult brothers and sisters are commonplace, but rarely discussed. When a men's group reaches a certain level of safety, this issue often emerges, and it's a painful one. These problems are usually long-standing, embarrassing and feel insoluble. Conflicts, roles and attitudes formed between children as they grow up in the original family can continue far into adult life. Think about your own family. Did the oldest sister boss the other kids around? Did the youngest son have it easy and escape his share of duties? Can you see the same patterns decades later and are they still resented? As Jane Mersky Leder, author of a book on this subject says, 'Our siblings push buttons that cast us in roles we felt sure we had let go of long ago: the baby, the peacekeeper, the caretaker, the avoider... It doesn't seem to matter how much time has elapsed or how far we've travelled.'

The solution which many families adopt is that siblings (ie brothers and sisters) keep their distance from each other, and relate with superficial politeness. This is why Christmas, weddings and funerals can be the scene of family upsets. When you have large numbers of the family together for an extended time, with alcohol loosening the restraints, buried tensions erupt. If you're a witness to such upsets, remember that the two mature adults in front of you are really only a few years old.

Jonathan's story

Jonathan is a friend of mine, now in his early sixties. He has one brother, Roger, four years younger. They are now good friends, but didn't grow up that way. Jonathan explained:

'When we were growing up, we hated each other. My parents gave me all the responsibilities and Roger was a spoilt, carefree brat, who didn't even respect me. When our father died ten years ago, our mother lost it for a while, so Roger and I had to collaborate in sorting out the estate, selling the family house and working out where our mother would live. We had three weeks of arguing about every single detail.

'Finally, in joint desperation, we started to talk about the dynamics between us. I told Roger how I'd felt about him in my childhood, and I realised I still felt that way. Roger told me that as a kid, he always found me arrogant, patronising, never taking him seriously, and he was still angry. We realised that we couldn't change the past, but simply naming what we felt, making the patterns visible, took most of the heat out of them. It also made us aware of the ways we habitually behaved to each other, and that awareness has changed the behaviour a lot – at least, most of the time. When one of us forgets, the other calls us on it pretty sharpish.'

Think about the roles and attitudes which you and your siblings took on in your childhood and teenage years. It's easier to blame the others, but recognise how your current behaviour and beliefs may continue the patterns. You alone cannot sweep away these habits, but if *you* change, it creates the possibility for others. Here are some hints on how to start the change:

◆ If you name the roles you still play and negative feelings you still carry towards your siblings, it creates a climate of honesty and a space where they can choose to do likewise. But don't expect an immediate matching response.

◆ When you and your siblings need to make a decision together, for example about care for your parents or selling the family home, suggest that you do it by consensus, treating everyone as equals. This can bring a more adult approach into the relations between you.

◆ When one of you needs to take a lead, suggest it should be the one with the most relevant skills and experience. Share tasks among you, for example in sorting out the estate after a parent has died. Again, this breaks old habits about who among the children should be responsible.

◆ Realise that you can influence your family dynamics, a bit. If your siblings are overemotional and always arguing, stay calm and adult. If they're always tight-lipped, let your own feelings show.

◆ If you have children of your own, look at the dynamics of your new family and compare them with your original one. Have some of the roles and attitudes passed down a generation? If so, do what you can to name them and clear this up with your children.

RESOURCES

You might think you could figure out family issues by common sense: I have found books on this subject surprisingly helpful. They can give you deeper understanding of what's going on, new skills and learning from other families' mistakes!

Ageing parents

You and Your Ageing Parents, by Claire Gillman. ISBN 978-0340864241. A clear and thoughtful book which considers both emotional and practical issues, for ageing parents and for their children, including drafting a will, using legal help and how to act as an executor.

What to Do When Someone Dies, by Anne Wadey. ISBN 978-1844901272. Gives a thorough explanation of how to register a death, who needs to be notified, how to organise the funeral, as well as applying for probate and sorting out tax, property and other financial matters.

Which? Legal Service: If your parents are happy to do things online, a simple and cheap way of making a will is to use a website such as www.whichwills.com. This is a legal service from Which? The online process is clear, simple and moderately priced.

When Parents Die, by Rebecca Abrams. ISBN 978-0722531310. A good book for handling the emotional impact of losing a parent. She emphasises how often bereaved people can feel isolation and lack of understanding from those around them. She describes how to handle the early days of grief, later stages of mourning, and the inner and outer changes and losses which need to be faced.

Between Mothers and Sons, by Evelyn Bassoff. ISBN 978-0452274624. There are surprisingly few books about the often tricky relationships between mothers and sons, and this is a carefully written, illuminating one. Written more from the viewpoint of mothers, and covers all life stages, but can be helpful for a man trying to understand what has been behind his mother's behaviour over the years.

Parenting adult children

Walking on Eggshells: Navigating the Delicate Relationship Between Adult Children and Parents, by Jane Isay. ISBN 978-0767920858. A thoughtful, readable book about negotiating the balance between your own needs and your adult children. Also, a useful American website for many family issues, including parenting adult children, is www.troubledwith.com.

Brothers and sisters

Why Can't We Get Along? Healing Adult Sibling Relationships, by Peter Goldenthal. ISBN 978-0471388425. This gently explains the kinds of issues that arise among brothers and sisters in childhood, and offers strategies to try to heal them in later adult life. He emphasises that one party alone cannot clear the problem: all you can do is try. Also has a useful section for spouses, partners and other innocent bystanders of such conflicts.

General

Families and how to Survive Them, by Robin Skynner and John Cleese. ISBN 978-0749314101. This book doesn't focus particularly on the maturing years, but it offers quite deep insights into the dynamics of couples, parenting and families, drawing on good sources in such areas as family therapy. First published in 1983, so some of it may seem a bit dated now, and the reference resources aren't current. Robin Skynner is a leading psychotherapist, and this book brings some complex ideas and professional approaches into a form which mainstream readers can understand – with some effort.

The Dance of Anger, by Harriet Lerner. ISBN 978-0722536230. Although written for women, this book is useful for anyone trying to understand and improve family dynamics by changing the way they handle their own anger and other family members'. Much of the book focuses on relationships within extended families.

Family Constellations: This is a powerful method to explore, understand and help clear difficult dynamics within your family, including negative patterns which may repeat across generations. It was developed by a German therapist, Bert Hellinger. Unfortunately there are many different websites for Constellations work. The only one I have personally used and can directly recommend is Judith Hemming, see www.movingconstellations.com. I suggest you ask friends who may recommend someone, or else surf around the websites and see who feels good for you. Just do a web search on 'Family Constellations UK'.

Chapter 7

Last Chance Saloon:
Addictions, anger, depression and alternatives

Reject your sense of injury and the injury itself disappears.
MARCUS AURELIUS

A sense of urgency and desperation seizes many men in their fifties: a feeling that time's running out, that their drive and reserves are depleted, a fear that old age is just around the next corner. For many men, these feelings shift by the late fifties, with a new sense of spaciousness and possibilities arising. However, by fifty, some men are deeply stuck in addiction or avoidance habits, and the fifties or early sixties are the last chance saloon: if you can't dig yourself out of these habits at this stage, you're probably stuck for the rest of your life. This chapter can help you explore your negative patterns and ways to shift them.

The focus of Chapter 5 is physical health, whereas this chapter looks at emotional and psychological issues. There are so many of these that I can only touch on a few. We all have short periods of feeling upset or downcast. This chapter can help you recognise longer-term problems which are damaging your happiness and can also affect your physical health. Maybe you have a condition which is already long-standing or a recent issue which could stay with you for years if you don't tackle it. In particular, this chapter takes a detailed look at how you can face up to and move through addictions, anxiety and avoidance, habitual anger and depression. It then takes a look at alternative medicines and therapies, which could be helpful for these situations and many others, and gives you guidelines on how to explore this area.

Nick is a man in his early fifties, who I knew vaguely through a singing group. He was never friendly with anyone and I noticed his clothes were getting grubby, and his face was red and blotchy. One evening we got talking and I was telling him about my work on this book. He looked uncomfortable, and then grunted 'Well, maybe you could help me. I've had problems with depression for a long time, but it's got much worse lately. I had a part-time job which was a kind of lifeline, but they shut the place down with all the sodded spending cuts.' He paused, and I felt him struggling with a terrible sense of shame. 'Yeah, I've started drinking a lot. On my own, I never did that before. And I'm hooked on computer games. Can't help it. My girlfriend put up with it all for a while, but dropped me last year. It's just bloody painful...'

Maybe you know men like this, maybe you are one. They're hard to reach because they're solitary and ashamed to admit their problems. My advice is, don't try to fix them, don't rush into solving their issue. Talking about your own problems will help them to trust you. Doing something social together that won't be demanding, like going for a walk, can help their morale. Hope that they'll open up to you about the problems, but even then, don't offer your solutions; instead try to help them find their own.

There are many possible shipwrecks in the maturing years: big events that force change upon you. Or you may have a sense of slowly sinking: for example, gradual decline in your health, your marriage, your circle of friends and so on. Big emotional issues can hit you now, even if your earlier years have been fairly cheerful. Many men keep so busy in their thirties and forties that they stave off problems that need facing. Beyond fifty, choose to deal with them. There's no need to feel alone, embarrassed or overwhelmed: these are normal issues and they can be solved.

I believe the basic crisis of life beyond fifty is a spiritual one: the need for meaning and purpose as death comes over the horizon. And the issues explored in this chapter could all be seen as symptoms of this underlying need. So you may want to read this chapter together with the following one, about dreams, dawns, dying and inspiration.

Are you feeling doubtful about reading this chapter, unsure that it has any relevance for you? This may be a sign that you need it more than most. One feature of addictions and avoidance is that people deny they have them or deny they're a difficulty. Admitting the problem and finding the willingness to change is a crucial first step. Check the facts: for example, how much alcohol are you consuming and what's the norm? There are good self-assessment tools for most of the issues in this chapter, listed in Resources.

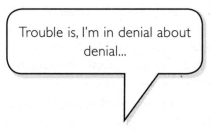

Trouble is, I'm in denial about denial...

Negative habits are there for a reason: usually so you can avoid some unbearable pain within you. The process of exploring and clearing these deep-set patterns is a tough one, like the Hero's Journey described in Chapter 2. It needs courage and persistence from you, and support from others. One place to start this process is by gently exploring what the pay-offs are to you from the habit. And can you guess at the pain underneath, which you are trying to avoid? Often this will be experiences in childhood and negative self-beliefs that you can't bear to live with. Your behaviour has been trying to shield you from this pain, but you need to decide that it's better to face the pain than continue a habit which is damaging you and people around you.

Six steps to making a difference

Whatever the issues you are trying to resolve, these six broad steps should help you:

1. *Get some facts.* Take an honest look at how much of the time you feel happy or not, and what the problems actually are. Keep a diary, maybe for a month, with as much factual detail as possible: for example, about addictive behaviour or how often you have felt depressed, anxious, lonely, and for how long each time? Keep a log of physical symptoms, like sleeplessness, indigestion or overeating, which may result from emotional issues.

2. *Initial research.* Use web searches, online self-tests, forums, phone helplines and relevant books to help you to define and diagnose your problem, explore ways to tackle it, and find people, organisations and other resources which could help you. Appreciate yourself for taking some action.

3. *Shortlist and investigate.* Make a shortlist of three specific initiatives you could take to clear your problem. For example, these could include doing a self-help programme, having counselling sessions, trying one of the complementary approaches described later or asking your GP to refer you for some treatment. Having made your shortlist, investigate each option carefully.

4. *Seek personal support.* Talk to a few close friends and family members, share your diary and your diagnosis with them, ask if they think you're being accurate or if there's anything they'd amend. Choose people who take a positive view and avoid ones who'll rubbish your capacity to change. Drinking partners and disappointed ex-girlfriends are *not* a good idea!

5. *Commit and stay with it.* Choose your preferred option from the shortlist, commit to it and stay with it through the programme. Discuss your intended plan with one or two close contacts before you commit, and ask for their support during the programme. If you really believe none of the three options

on your shortlist would suit you, go through the process again. If the second go-round produces nothing you're willing to try, admit that there is strong resistance and avoidance on your part, and seek some professional help.

6. Review. When you make your commitment, set yourself goals for the changes you want and the time in which you want to achieve them. Review your progress regularly: this is best done with a friend or professional, and also review at the end of your programme.

Partners with problems

Perhaps it's your partner who's suffering from long-term depression, addiction, anxiety or whatever. One writer uses the term de-selfing to describe how partners of people with addiction or other major issues can focus their life on the partner and the problem, losing their own sense of self and much of the pleasure in life. Addiction recovery programmes use the term *co-addicts* to highlight the ways that partners of addicts get trapped in dependent patterns, which can also be a form of addiction. If you're in a situation like this, you may have some painful choices to make. Where do you draw the line? How often do you set an ultimatum and extend it? Where do you balance your needs to get a life with your love for your partner, your desire to help her recover? There are no simple answers.

Many of the organisations, websites and books mentioned in Resources offer advice and support for partners, and some of the processes in this chapter may be relevant for you too. If your partner is receiving professional help, ask this person what resources are available for you. If your partner remains in denial, ignores your concerns and refuses to seek help, you may need to leave the relationship. Ironically, that is sometimes the crisis that forces the partner to face the situation.

The healing of forgiveness

If you dig underneath many of the challenges which this chapter explores, you'll probably find the desire to punish. Subconsciously, these behaviours are a way of getting back at people who've hurt us, or of punishing ourselves.

I found that some of my depressed periods were driven by anger at my parents, and a desire to hurt them by showing them that I was *still* suffering for the mistakes they had made in my childhood. I hadn't been aware of my motives and I hadn't told my folks, so the only loser was me. If you find yourself sliding into addiction, anger or depression after an external shock like divorce or redundancy, you may be trying to punish the person who hurt you, like your wife or your boss.

Look at your own situation and take time to dig down into the feelings beneath it. Are you getting at someone else? Or punishing yourself? The logic for this is that if bad things happen to you, you must be bad, so you deserve to be punished. It's another repeating pattern.

A crucial step to clearing these feelings and the damaging behaviours they create is forgiveness. You probably need to forgive other people *and* yourself. Both can be hard: I still struggle with this. It may help to look at the different voices within you, using the methods in Chapter 2. The punishing parts of you are probably the Hurt Child, the Inner Judge and the Negative Parent. Acknowledge their feelings, but seek the voice of your heart and your higher self. Find compassion for all of you.

This extended version of the Lord's Prayer line about *Forgive us our trespasses*, by Neil Douglas-Klotz in *Prayers of the Cosmos*, has helped me:

> *Loose the cords of mistakes binding us,*
> *as we release the strands we hold*
> *of others' guilt.*
>
> *Forgive our hidden past, the secret shames,*
> *as we consistently forgive*
> *what others hide.*

Lighten our load of secret debts as
we relieve others of their
need to repay.

Erase the inner marks our failures make,
just as we scrub our hearts
of others' faults.

ADDICTIONS? NOT ME...

Addictions come in many forms, such as alcohol, drugs or sex, internet porn or gaming. Any of these can be life-destroying. This field is confusing because the substances or activities which are destructive addictions for some men are enjoyed by others. So how do you know if you're addicted? If you already feel reluctant to read more, if a speech of angry denial is welling up about the mere idea that you could be hooked, if you're cross because this is no one's business but your own, these are danger signs. Another is if you feel lonely and find it hard to have real contact even with your family and others who should be close to you.

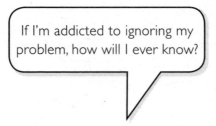

If I'm addicted to ignoring my problem, how will I ever know?

An addiction is a repeated habitual pattern so strong that the physical or emotional impact of stopping is unbearable. To the addict, his behaviour feels normal, essential, the point around which his life revolves. Addictions are the most extreme form of avoidance, an attempt to escape some deeper pain which we can't bear to face. If you're struggling with addiction, see it as a call to face some major hurt you've been avoiding. Chapter 2 should help you with this, and later sections of this chapter.

In his book *Facing the Shadow,* Patrick Carnes explains that an addiction starts when a habit takes over and dominates our behaviour, becoming an obsession or compulsion. He states that: 'An addiction is a pathological relationship with mood–altering experience; it happens when we have lost the ability to choose about certain behaviours. Since it is a progressive condition, addiction eventually leads the addict to sacrifice everything else in spite of his/her growing sense of despair.'

Often what persuades an addict to admit his problem and seek help is a crisis. If your partner wants to leave, if health is going downhill, if you're struggling to keep the job or you get over your head in debt, you have a serious problem which could be caused by addiction. Although the crisis may be external, you have to want to change *for yourself.* A friend of mine who is a drug rehab professional told me, 'If a man comes to me because his wife is threatening to leave, I wouldn't take it any further. Breaking an addiction requires huge courage and commitment, which has to start with the addict.'

If you need help to clarify if you have an addiction problem, here are four steps you can take:

1. Use the screening questionnaire in Appendix 2.

2. Call a specialised helpline (see Resources).

3. Make an appointment to talk to your GP, who can refer you to a wide range of services to help with diagnosis, treatment and support.

4. Ask a couple of close friends or family members if they believe you may have an addiction problem and if they are willing to support you in breaking it.

If you're fighting an addiction, you need to recognise the difference between abstinence and recovery. Abstinence means just stopping: this is something you may do by willpower, but it rarely lasts for long. Recovery means facing the core pain:

feeling the hurt, then moving on from a sense of childlike help-lessness to taking responsibility for yourself and your choices here and now. There are various programmes designed to guide and support you through this journey of recovery.

> **The best teachers lived their nightmare to find their dream.**

What lies beyond recovery can be fulfilling for you and of deep benefit to others. I know several maturing men who are recovered addicts, and are great teachers and role models for other men, including young men who are badly lost. If you've been down at the bottom yourself, you have credibility and a unique gift to offer others when you recover. As you go through this process, form a vision of what you want in your life when you get back the time, energy and ability to choose. This vision can keep you going through the bumpy bits.

Addiction treatment

Addictions vary hugely in their severity, and their impact on you and people around you. This section is not a professional guide to treating addiction, but offers general guidelines. You'll find further help in Resources. Even if you think your addiction is minor, take the first two steps below, since that will ensure you have an objective view about the seriousness of the problem and how to treat it.

One of the best-known addiction recovery programmes is Twelve Step, pioneered by Alcoholics Anonymous, and now offered by organisations for a large range of other addictions. It has helped many people, but won't suit everyone. Twelve Step organisations can be prescriptive and may lead people into dependency on them.

Step 1: Face the facts. Are your health and close relationships going downhill? If you might be overusing a substance, like alcohol or drugs, how much are you actually consuming? Keep a Drinks Diary or similar – see under NHS in Resources. If you're hooked on an activity, like gaming or porn, how many hours per week is it taking up? Include both the time for the activity and all the related time, fantasising, getting the money and setting up sessions.

Step 2: See your GP. The National Health Service recommend your GP as the start point in diagnosing and treating addiction. GPs have access to a range of resources and can refer you on the NHS to specialist services and treatment. For example, the NHS offers a Sensible Drinking programme, which is a self-help process with professional support.

Step 3: Do an online search to find an organisation relevant to your addiction. There are support network organisations for a huge number of addictions. The websites themselves will give you a lot of information, and usually enable you to contact experienced volunteer helpers and mentors, professional help and support groups.

Step 4: Evolve a support network to help you with your recovery process. It's really tough breaking an addiction. In organisations like Alcoholics Anonymous, you have a personal mentor who is a recovered addict committed to being there for you, and meetings with other recovering addicts are a crucial part of the process. Most recovery networks offer you the chance of regular support groups with other recovering addicts.

Step 5: Involve family, friends and colleagues. Try to find a small number of close friends or family members who are willing to offer you active support and who you can talk to regularly on your journey of recovery. Your family, friends and work colleagues may be supportive of your intention to break the addiction or may already have lost patience with you. Either way, tell them what you're doing, tell them of your commitment and ask for any support you need, which may include not asking you out for a drink or a smoke, or whatever the addiction is.

ANXIETY AND AVOIDANCE

This section offers help with problems which may be spoiling your life if they're severe and ongoing. When you feel exhausted and despairing about a long-term condition, it's hard to find the energy to change. If you go on as you are, will you have the energy to tackle this in five years' time? Or ten? Believing you're in the last chance saloon, right now, may help you take a step. If you can just make a first move, you'll find there are people and treatments which can help you. Keep believing your life can be better.

Some of the methods suggested are similar to those elsewhere in this chapter, so please forgive a bit of overlap. You'll also find other parts of this chapter relevant to problems like anxiety and avoidance: for example, the Six Steps at the start, and the alternative approaches near the end.

Anxiety: Is it getting on your nerves?

Anxiety is a hard topic to cover, since it takes so many forms and overlaps with many other conditions. For example, panic attacks, agoraphobia and other strong aversions are sometimes seen as forms of anxiety. On the other hand, we all get a bit anxious sometimes. Some of the signs of a major anxiety problem would be:

◆ It is seriously affecting your daily life, for example work, family and social contacts.

◆ You worry often and uncontrollably.

◆ You frequently feel stressed and upset by your anxieties.

◆ You are anxious about many things and often fear a bad outcome.

If your anxiety might be serious, get a diagnosis from a professional, since there are so many types of anxiety and treatments will vary. Forms of treatment include self-help programmes, support groups and specialised therapy or counselling. To get a diagnosis, you could see your GP or contact one of the specialist anxiety support organisations listed in Resources. Anxiety has serious physical effects as well as emotional. It can weaken your immune system, cause high blood pressure and digestion trouble. It can also lead to problems with sexual performance, which can crank up the anxiety even more. As with depression, exercise, good diet, vitamins and minerals can all help your recovery.

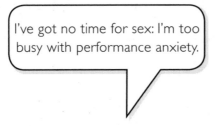

I've got no time for sex: I'm too busy with performance anxiety.

Avoidance

We all use avoidance to some extent: it's the range of ways we *try* to reduce contact with feelings, people or situations we find difficult. The question is whether your avoidance activities are so time-consuming and long-running that they're a major feature of your life.

For example, you may spend three nights a week playing internet games or watching old movies. You may tell yourself it's because you haven't got over your wife leaving or you're depressed. Ask yourself, are you really *enjoying* these activities? How long have you been doing them? Do they enrich your life? You may be trying to shield yourself from pain, but you could be trapped in avoidance. If you can gather the will, courage and skills to face the pain, you free yourself to move forward and choose what you want for the future.

Avoidance plays a significant part in other problems explored in this chapter. If you're avoiding feelings *within* you, this can lead to depression or addiction. If you're avoiding *external* situations or other people, this can cause anxiety.

If your avoidance habit is deep-rooted and long-running, this suggests you feel a lot of fear and pain about facing something or someone. But often, the situations we fear most have the greatest healing or learning potential. For many men, the greatest terror is losing control, surrender – especially to a woman. The biggest thing I learned from several years of tantra training is that surrender to the woman is the *crucial step in reaching true manhood*. Without this surrender, you get macho men, hollow shells running away from their fears. If you have a loving partner and good support, facing your avoidance can bring you through to a masculine quality that knows its weakness and its strength, and is open to the feminine.

Don't be casual about facing something big like a major avoidance pattern: talk it through with a counsellor, a friend or a healer. If there are skills you need, such as conflict resolution, learn them. What you're avoiding may be your own painful feelings: the processes in Chapter 2 can be helpful with these. Maybe you need closer friends and a stronger social network: these are covered in Chapter 9.

ANGER: EXIT THE TRAGEDY

The effects of habitual anger are tragic for the angry man and those around him. He will become more isolated, beset by problems at work and home which intensify the vicious circle, deepening the low self-confidence, the sense of guilt, shame and incompetence, which mean that small issues lead to intense anger. Those around him become more guarded, fearful and angry: partners and kids are often the most abused and damaged.

This is tragic because the roots of habitual anger are often set in childhood. You may believe you're angry because your parents or others were abusively angry to you. It's true that we often repeat the behaviours we suffered from in childhood. You may feel like a victim, you can point to what 'caused' your anger. And you may now be stuck in a mesh of limiting beliefs and damaging behaviours that's hard to escape from. But believing you're a helpless figure in a tragic situation is never going to move you on. You have to find the will to take a first step and then there's plenty of help on the journey. Many men have found the exit from this tragedy, so believe you can too.

I'm only angry because
my dad was.

Habitual anger may be linked to a range of other problems, such as:

- Addiction, especially to alcohol, which raises the intensity of anger.

- Depression.

- Physical ailments, such as ulcers and digestive disorders, and heart disease.

- Difficulty expressing feelings and hearing others.

- High need for control, finding change and uncertainty difficult.

- Low self-esteem, reluctance to admit problems and seek help.

If some of this applies to you, don't despair and don't throw this book on the fire. There are well-proven ways to clear all these problems and more.

The first step is to assess how severe your anger problem is. The Novaco Anger Inventory (see Resources) is a simple self-test process. If this shows a severe situation, or if your anger is ever violent, seek professional help urgently. For less severe anger, you may want to try a self-help approach, perhaps combined with a mutual support group. You can find references for these in Resources. If you have several related problems and don't know where to start, get professional advice, for example by seeing your GP and asking for a referral.

This section is not an anger-management programme, but here are some examples of the methods such programmes may use:

Befriend yourself. Stop the habit of constantly criticising and blaming yourself. Admit your faults, but also your good points. Don't generalise one mistake to feeling you're a worthless man.

Open up to happiness. Angry men don't believe they deserve to be happy and can't relax enough to enjoy themselves. You *can* change this, but you need to believe it's possible.

Recognise and challenge your distorted beliefs. Keeping an anger diary, as in the book *Beyond Anger,* can help you see the habitual prejudices about yourself and others which fuel your anger, such as 'he's out to get me', or 'I'm no use to anyone'.

Pre-plan handling difficult situations. Certain people and situations may be flashpoints for your anger. Understand why and work out in advance how to handle them – for example, telling a joke against yourself may stop someone who keeps teasing you.

Stop seeing conversations as conflicts. Because of low self-confidence, angry men feel they need to 'win' in conversations, ie their opinion must prevail. Practise discussing instead of competing.

Use assertiveness methods to meet your needs. Anger often flares up if a man can't express his needs. Assertiveness, also discussed in Chapter 3, is a set of simple methods which enable you to say what you want, without losing your temper.

Review your role in negative family dynamics. If you're habitually angry, this may link with angry parents or a wife who has 'de-selfed' and taken responsibility for your problems. You need to understand such dynamics, and change the beliefs and behaviours in you which contribute to them – realising that you can't make anyone else change.

DEPRESSION, AND GETTING OVER IT

Depression is one of the biggest problems for men beyond fifty. We all feel low sometimes, but depression is long-term – I've met many mature men who have been depressed for years, often on antidepressants long-term, and are resigned to living in semi-gloom indefinitely. Many of these men are isolated, almost invisible.

How would you know if you're depressed? Typical symptoms are self-dislike, lack of motivation, loss of appetite or overeating, being preoccupied with negative thoughts and feelings about yourself and the world, loss of energy, sleeping poorly, pessimism, lack of interest in other people and life in general, and thinking about dying or hurting yourself.

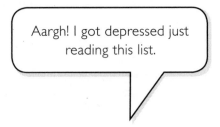

Aargh! I got depressed just reading this list.

Typical causes of depression are feelings of anger, guilt or anxiety. Often one event starts it, but we generalise to believe we are worthless/the world hates us/life is dangerous, and so on. It may help you to realise that depression is *not* a biological illness that you catch, nor is it genetic and inherited from parents. It's about your responses, which can be changed. When you feel depressed, it's hard to believe things could ever be better, difficult to find energy to take an initiative. Whatever you try, believe you *can* get over depression, you don't have to go on like this. The best approaches combine some self-help with professional support.

Since depression is a widespread problem, it's understandable that there are large numbers of techniques, medications and therapies which claim to clear it, and many of these contradict each other. Doing a web search on this topic is enough to leave anyone depressed! There's a wide range of methods which have worked for some men – ask your contacts what has worked for them. One of the methods with the best-proven record of lifting depression is CBT, which stands for Cognitive Behavioural Therapy. You'll find a good self-help book using CBT listed in Resources, and a GP might refer you to a therapist trained in this method. CBT is well suited to men since its focus is on changing behaviours through tangible, practical actions.

Antidepressants can play a valuable role, especially if your depression is so severe that you can't cope with everyday life. However, it's important to avoid becoming dependent on them: six to eighteen months is a reasonable period of treatment, and coming off them needs handling with care.

An interesting feature of depression treatment in recent years has been the use of meditation and the evidence of its effectiveness. The best-selling US book on depression, listed in Resources, uses meditation, breathwork and relaxation exercises as central approaches. I have been meditating regularly since my thirties and it has helped me to centre on the positive and on the bigger picture, instead of identifying with my pain and isolation.

Depression is often linked to loneliness. If you are isolating yourself, this is a sign that you need to get help with your condition, as the solitude can lead to suicide. My father was depressed for much of his adult life, and on antidepressants for many years. I've had several periods of depression: one of the worst was after my fiftieth birthday, when I had split up with my wife, moved out of the family home and my main consulting client ended our contract. The approach which helped me out of this is called Human Givens. It takes a straightforward, positive approach working with tangibles like breathing and relaxation, as well as visualisation of successful outcomes.

For help in diagnosing and treating depression, through

Human Givens or other methods, see Resources. Here's a summary of main elements in the Human Givens approach:

◆ *Relaxation.* Depression is a vicious circle – you feel stressed and anxious, so you can't sleep well, which makes you more stressed and anxious... There are simple breathing and other relaxation methods which can change this pattern, help you feel calmer and see things in perspective.

◆ *Understand your needs.* The term Human Givens means basic needs we must meet to feel happy. Knowing and naming your needs is a first step to meeting them.

◆ *Take small practical steps forward.* If you're depressed, there's not much point setting huge goals like stopping smoking or learning the violin. Set a few small, realistic goals and build up your confidence from there.

◆ *Reframe negative beliefs.* Depressed people generalise any negative event into a universal negative belief, such as 'nobody likes me'. There are methods to change this self-destructive habit.

◆ *Laughter is a great healer.* Simple as that!

◆ *Visualise success.* Instead of being anxious and pessimistic about a future event, like a blind date, picturing a future event positively can help to make it happen that way.

◆ *Take physical exercise.* Research shows that exercise and daylight help to reduce depression, but choose a form of exercise you enjoy.

◆ *Diet and vitamins can help.* Some kinds of food and drink (especially alcohol) can increase depression, while others can reduce it. There are also several vitamins, such as Omega-3 fish oils, which have been proven helpful. For more on this, see the Patrick Holford book in Resources.

As you start to gain confidence and momentum in your recovery, you may find material in other chapters helpful, for example on relationship skills (Chapter 3), new approaches to work and money (Chapter 4), and finding new social skills and friends (Chapter 9).

ALTERNATIVE APPROACHES

This is a huge, loosely defined field which could include products like herbal remedies, hands-on therapies like kinesiology and various forms of spiritual healing. Alternative therapies are sometimes defined as anything which is not classed as conventional medicine, but the boundaries are blurry. Some approaches which used to be seen as alternative now have a professional structure, research evidence and acceptance by some conventional medicos. Others are unregulated and some are pretty flaky.

Some alternative therapies are relevant for the kinds of emotional, mental or psychological problems covered in this chapter. Others will address the physical ailments in Chapter 5. I've used various alternative treatments and know many others who have: sometimes really helpful, sometimes unproven, more rarely a waste of time. A web search for alternative therapies will throw up fifty million entries: it's such a vast field that I won't try to give an overview. You'll find some tools in Resources to help with that.

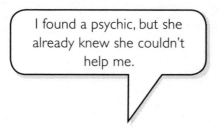

I found a psychic, but she already knew she couldn't help me.

Another term for this area is complementary medicine, suggesting that these approaches can be used alongside conventional medical treatments. Surveys in the UK and elsewhere show that over 30% of cancer patients used some form of complementary or alternative medicine. If you want to explore alternative approaches, here are some basic tips:

◆ Ask friends about treatments and individual therapists who have helped them with similar problems. Get a personal recommendation if possible.

◆ Find an organisation specialising in help with your condition, such as those listed in Resources. Check their website, ask their support groups or professional advisors if there are alternative therapies they believe could be helpful and ask how to check them out.

◆ Do a web search on any therapy or product you are considering. See if there is a professional organisation, what its rules for qualification are and whether it looks reliable. Look for feedback from users.

◆ Before committing to a treatment, have an exploratory meeting with the therapist or a chat with the supplier. Ask about benefits, risks, codes of conduct and standards you should expect.

You could see all the conditions covered in this chapter as arising from a need for emotional and spiritual healing: clearing or lightening a deep emotional wound, and finding a sense of meaning and purpose in life. A few of the alternative therapies that could help are:

Ayurveda. A traditional Indian system that treats mind, body and spirit as integrated. Treatments could involve herbal remedies, dietary regimes, massage and other methods.

Bach essences. Using diluted essences from plants, especially for emotional and mental challenges.

Craniosacral therapy. A gentle hands-on therapy which works with subtle movements of fluids and tissues, helping to clear emotional, psychological or physical stresses.

Herbal remedies. These may be based on Chinese or Western systems. A practitioner will assess your condition and prescribe a remedy tailored to it.

Homeopathy. A system of medicine using highly diluted substances to trigger the body's natural system of healing. The diagnosis by the homeopath is typically quite thorough and subtle, and usually involves exploring emotional and psychological issues as well as physical ones.

Spiritual healing. This is a huge field in its own right. Various methods are used to bring spiritual energy to support the client, strengthen their own life energy and clear blockages.

RESOURCES

This chapter includes some of the most difficult challenges in the whole book, and they definitely need outside help. Using websites and telephone helplines to find relevant organisations and professional support may be the best place to start.

Addictions

Most of the recommended resources for this topic are websites, since this is the best way of getting information for a specific addiction and for your local area. However, there are some good books too:

No Big Deal: A Guide to Recovery from Addictions, by John Coats. ISBN 978-0955367700. This is based on the Twelve-Step process, probably the most widely used method for addiction recovery. Written in clear, commonsense language and can be used as a self-help process, or if you are working with a Twelve-Step organisation such as Alcoholics Anonymous.

A Gentle Path Through the Twelve Steps, by Patrick Carnes. ISBN 978-1592858439. A beautifully written workbook, using the Twelve-Step process to help recovery from a range of addictions. Also suitable for co-addicts. Carnes comments that some recovering addicts take the same compulsive approach to recovery as they did to addiction: this book offers a truly supportive, gentle approach.

Out of the Shadows: Understanding Sexual Addiction, by Patrick Carnes. ISBN 978-1568386218. A clear, compassionate and practical book on a complex and difficult topic. Good for understanding the issue for yourself and your family, using the Twelve-Step process.

Beating Addictions: A good website to start with, easy to navigate and has large amounts of useful content. It covers addictions of all levels of severity. See: www.beatingaddictions.co.uk.

NHS Choices: This is a huge website, with lots of valuable information on addiction recovery. It includes explanations of how to seek help, typical kinds of treatment and a local search function for details of relevant organisations in your area. See: www.nhs.uk.

Alcoholics Anonymous: This has a wide range of useful information and contacts, and also a good diagnostic questionnaire. See: www.alcoholics-anonymous.org.uk.

If you are fighting addiction to any specific substance or activity, a web search is pretty certain to identify an organisation which can help you with recovery. Many of these have online support networks, as well as phone lines and facilities to meet with an individual mentor or other recovering addicts for support.

Anxiety

Free yourself from anxiety, by Emma Fletcher and Martha Langley. ISBN 978-1845283117. A self-help guide which will help you understand many types of anxiety disorder, how to get a professional diagnosis and work with a helper, good self-help advice, plus pointers on diet, exercise and lots more.

Overcoming anxiety, by Helen Kennerley. ISBN 978-1849010719. Part of a series of self-help books using Cognitive Behavioural Therapy (CBT), one of the most widely used therapies. It's clearly written and will give you an understanding of the problem, as well as clear guidance on methods to overcome it.

There are several good websites which can help you understand the different forms of anxiety and get help with diagnosis and treatment, for example: www.anxietycare.org.uk and www.anxietyalliance.org.uk.

If you search for 'GAD-7' on www.serene.me.uk, you'll find a self-assessment questionnaire for General Anxiety Disorder.

If you go to www.nhs.uk and search under 'anxiety', you'll find a range of briefing information and links to other support organisations.

Anger

Beyond Anger: A Guide for Men, by Thomas J. Harbin. ISBN 978-1569246214. An excellent book by an American therapist who specialises in working with angry men. It's very clear in showing the sources of anger and the ways it distorts men's beliefs. A down-to-earth self-help guide to changing angry behaviour.

Overcoming Anger and Irritability, by William Davies. ISBN 978-1849011310. This is a highly rated UK self-help guide, based on Cognitive Behavioural Therapy, one of the most widely used methods for treating anger, depression and other issues. Clear, practical and easy to follow. Different from the above recommended book, since this is for anyone, not just men, and it covers various levels of anger and irritability, whereas the other book is focused on severe, habitual anger.

Mind: If you search under 'anger' on this website, you'll find a good general briefing and a list of relevant organisations. See: www.mind.org.uk.

NHS Choices: Search under 'anger management' for a useful list of self-help techniques and a range of links. The NHS recommends that you start by seeing your GP who can advise on appropriate treatment. This could be on a self-help basis. There are also some NHS-funded anger-management courses. See: www.nhs.uk.

See www.counsellingteam.com or do a web search to find the Novaco Anger Inventory. This is a widely used self-test to assess the degree of anger problems.

SupportLine: A telephone support line and website run by a UK charity, which offers telephone support and information for anger management and many problems. The website includes self-help methods, guidance on finding support, and links to relevant organisations and websites. See: www.supportline.org.uk.

Also consider adult education courses on anger management. These *could* be good and reasonably priced.

Depression, and getting over it

How to Lift Depression... Fast, by Joe Griffin and Ivan Tyrrell. ISBN 978-1899398416. Based on the Human Givens approach, this is my preferred book on the subject. Clear, constructive, very useable on a self-help basis, although it does recommend working with a Human Givens therapist (see website below).

Overcoming Depression: A Self-help Guide Using Cognitive Behavioural Techniques, by Paul Gilbert. ISBN 978-1849010665. Cognitive Behavioural Therapy is widely used for depression and other problems, and GPs will often refer people to a CBT practitioner. This book is intended as a self-help manual.

The Mindful Way Through Depression, by Mark Williams and others. ISBN 978-1593851286. Amazon lists this as the best-selling book in the US on depression, and its focus is on a set of techniques, including breathing and meditation, which now have a good medical research pedigree. The UK edition of the book includes a CD of related guided meditations.

New Optimum Nutrition for the Mind, by Patrick Holford. ISBN 978-1591202592. A helpful book on ways that diet, vitamins and minerals can help combat depression, anxiety, memory problems and other issues, from one of the UK's top nutritionists. It gives clear explanations of how alcohol, stress and poor diet affect mood and mind, and why his recommendations can help.

Human Givens: If you want to learn more about the Human Givens approach generally and find a therapist trained in this method in your area, see www.humangivens.com.

DepressionAlliance: This UK charity offers a range of publications, many of them free downloads, and several ways to understand possible treatments and make a choice. They also offer various types of support, such as self-help groups, an online support forum and volunteer helpers. You can find a wide array of information and resources at www.depressionalliance.org.

Serenity Programme: If you search for 'PHQ-9' on www.serene.me.uk or other sites, you'll access a self-assessment questionnaire for depression.

Rethink Mental Illness: For a good general briefing, download the depression facts sheet on www.rethink.org. This has a helpful list of symptoms, explains various forms of depression and lists a range of typical treatments. They also offer an advice and information service by phone or email.

Alternative approaches

Natural Therapy Pages: This covers a good range of therapies. You can search for local practitioners for any specified therapy. See: www.naturaltherapypages.co.uk.

Ayurveda

There are various schools or branches of Ayurveda, so it can be a complex field. Here are a couple of ways into it:

Maharishi Ayurveda: One of the leading Ayurveda organisations internationally: I have used them in the UK and can recommend them personally. See: www.maharishi.co.uk.

Ayurvedic Practitioners Association: This UK association enables you to find practitioners and therapists in your area. See: www.apa.uk.com.

Bach flower remedies

This field is also complicated: there are numerous outlets supplying these remedies. Also there are now many different ranges of flower and other essences as well as the Bach ones.

The Bach Centre: Based at the cottage in Oxfordshire where Edward Bach developed the remedies. Through their website you can contact a registered practitioner in your area or have a phone or personal consultation with staff at the centre. See: www.bachcentre.com.

Bach Flower Remedies: This website includes a useful online tool which suggests remedies for common emotional issues plus information about the remedies. See: www.bach–flowers.co.uk.

Craniosacral therapy

Craniosacral Therapy Association: Provides information on what this therapy is and enables you to find qualified local practitioners. See: www.craniosacral.co.uk.

Herbal remedies

National Institute of Medical Herbalists: This website provides briefing about herbal medicine and how it can help a range of conditions, plus facilities to find local practitioners. See: www.nimh.org.uk.

Homeopathy

The Society of Homeopaths: This provides an explanation of homeopathy and links to find a local practitioner. See: www. homeopathy-soh.org.

Spiritual healing

A web search on this topic yields nearly ten million entries. There are a lot of individual healers who are not part of an organisation, don't have formal training and would regard these as irrelevant. This is definitely an area to look for personal recommendations and check people out before you make commitments. One place to start is www.thehealingtrust.org. uk. This is the largest organisation of spiritual healers in the UK: the umbrella body is a charitable trust and non-denominational. Its members have to meet minimum training standards, comply with a professional code of conduct and carry professional insurance. Through their website you can find local healers and information about local healing centres.

Chapter 8

Dreams, dawns, dying and inspiration

Here is a test to find whether your mission on Earth is finished: if you're alive, it isn't.

RICHARD BACH

The last chapter looked at clearing the shadows; this one is about bringing more light into your life, and finding a sense of purpose and inspiration. That may sound grand, but it doesn't need to be: if you can find a sense of purpose for tomorrow, or next week, it's progress. You could choose to help a friend or try a morning volunteering: small steps are a vital start. Especially if you're digging yourself out of depression or other major problems, finding purpose and meaning even on a small scale will lift your mood and move you forward.

This chapter explores various ways of finding inspiration, and bringing a sense of opening up and new dawns into your life. You may be surprised to see dying covered here: facing up to death can really help you to value life and enjoy it fully. This chapter also explores how a spiritual path and practice could help you, and how time in nature can be a deep source of inspiration and understanding.

One of the biggest pleasures in my life over the past fifteen years has been seeing many men over fifty emerging from their pain, finding a sense of pleasure and purpose again – including myself. This may be a zigzag journey, with many ups and downs, but have faith: it does happen.

> **Can you dream of going to a football match, without dreaming of the result?**

DREAMS FOR AWAKENING

We use the word 'dreams' to mean many things. There are ordinary dreams that we have at night. Then there are nostalgic fantasies, as in the poignant Roy Orbison song, *In Dreams*, about a man whose actual life is bleak, and who only lives in his dreams of the woman he loved. And there are daydreams, happy imaginings which fill the time pleasantly. All kinds of dreams can show you what you long for, but this section will focus on conscious dreams which can give you motivation and direction. This means using the right side of the brain, which is good at intuition and creativity, whereas many men use mostly the left side, which is strong on logic, analysis and solving detailed problems.

So in this section, let's say that a dream is a vision which excites you, and which you'd feel happy if you could fulfil. It could be large or small. I had a dream for several weeks of going to a Premier League football match with some friends; it's a superb tribal experience and a great thing to share with mates. On a bigger scale, I've carried the dream of this book for many months. It's been hard work to achieve this dream, but my belief that it would help many men and be satisfying for me kept me going.

So a dream could take little effort or lots to make it real. It could take hours or years, it could help just you or many people. Your dream could be a new relationship or a new shirt. It could be helping to save the planet or brightening your back yard. Fulfilling any of these dreams would lift you, expand you, enrich your life and get you moving forward.

One step towards finding such a dream is to observe your ordinary night-time dreams and daytime fantasies. What are you longing for? Maybe your fantasy is to be a rock singer or end world poverty. Perhaps your dream is to get your full health back or find a happy relationship. Try to picture your dream and then dig under these images: what's the *feeling* you want? Is it being appreciated, feeling fulfilled, finding real love? Often the form of the fantasy is misleading, shaped by media hype, but there may be something real beneath it.

A second step is to *call for a dream*. In order to find a vision, you really have to want it and you have to be willing to receive it. Some people are so unconfident or so scared of change that they don't want even positive challenges. If you're up for an adventure, say out loud, 'I'm calling for a vision': this tells your intuition, your subconscious and your higher self that you're willing to hear them. And if you want a dream for a particular aspect of your life, name it, put the word out. Check that you're truly open to fulfilling your dream: imagine it coming true and see if you have any fears or resistances about this. If so, the processes in Chapters 2 and 7 can help you.

Dreams have their own timing, so be patient about the response to your call. When a dream shows up, be welcoming, even if it seems strange or hard to understand. Give yourself time to interpret the message. And if no dream comes, ask yourself: was I ready, was I willing to receive it? Maybe you have some more preparation to do, such as facing fears or clearing negative beliefs.

The third step, when you have a dream, large or small, is to *picture yourself achieving your vision*. Believe you can do it, and enjoy it. Tim Smit, who created the Eden Project, says that the Tinkerbell principle (as in *Peter Pan*) was vital in his success: you have to believe in a vision before it can happen.

SPIRITUAL DAWNS: WORTH A TRY

For some men beyond fifty, their spiritual path is a vital inspiration, a way of keeping centred, and a big resource in facing problems. For others, the very idea is threatening or meaningless. I'm in the first of these groups and I have friends in both of them. You should make your own choices, but if you don't have a spiritual path, it's worth exploring the possibility and seeing if it could help you.

If you're hostile or sceptical about this topic, ask yourself why. Are you confusing organised religion or cult gurus with spirituality? Are you alarmed at the idea that there's some power beyond the individual? Trust that you won't be conned or brainwashed: give it a try.

The term *spiritual path* means a set of beliefs and values, and a spiritual practice means ways that you affirm and anchor them. Typically, the central belief is in some power or presence which is not material or measurable, which is bigger than individuals. My path combines elements from several traditions, especially Christian, Buddhist, Celtic and Sufi. A key Sufi belief is that there is a divine presence in all forms of life, so we are all part of divine unity.

One of the ways my spiritual path helps me is when I am upset or overwhelmed. Instead of being completely identified with the hurting part of me, which is usually the inner child, I can find my connection with my higher self: the divine spark in me, which connects to the divine spark in all life. Another way it helps is in finding direction and purpose. I believe we each have a soul that chooses the life we come into, including its blessings and problems. One of my most frequent prayers is to ask to be guided so that my soul can serve the highest good of all and align with divine purpose: this is the prayer explained on page 134.

In his excellent book, *The Power of Modern Spirituality*, William Bloom poses three questions that can help you recognise the spiritual aspects already in your life:

◆ *In what kind of circumstances do you most easily connect with the wonder and energy of nature and all existence, and feel your heart touched and your consciousness awakened?*

◆ *When is it easiest for you to retreat from activity, pause and reflect on your life, so as to manage your life and next steps?*

◆ *What are your highest values and how do you express them as a form of service for the community of life?*

He goes on to suggest three behaviours at the heart of all spiritual paths, whether or not these fit within a named tradition:

◆ *Connection.* Sometimes, surely, your heart is touched and you connect with the wonder and energy of life.

◆ *Reflection.* Sometimes already, you pause and reflect on your life and actions, and ponder how to change and improve.

◆ *Service.* And sometimes, of course, you have a clear sense of what is right and what is wrong, and you act so as to do good for others.

Maybe you've had a bad experience with organised religion. There are priests who abuse their position and organisations who may manipulate you with guilt or shame. Don't let this cut you off from the deep wisdom and superb teachers you can find in many religions and other, less formal spiritual paths. If you are wary of being told what to do, explore paths like Buddhism, Sufism, Quakerism and Unitarianism.

The set of values in a spiritual path could be a code that's set down, like a Christian creed or Buddhist precepts. The Twelve Steps, mentioned in Chapter 7, are a spiritual path, with a code. However, many people evolve their own set of values. Either way makes you more aware of how you want to live and of the positive or negative effect you can have on other people. Choosing and naming your values and affirming them regularly can help you to live by them.

> **The best prayer is to ask what to pray for.**

A spiritual practice can take many forms. Going to a church service or a meditation group is one. I find it's helpful to do some practice daily, so I start with a half-hour of silent medita-tion and prayers every morning. Some spiritual paths include a periodic review with a mentor, who can help you take stock of your progress and can suggest specific practices. When I started my Sufi path, I was struggling with low self-confidence and my mentor suggested using sound mantras to affirm the positive qualities I needed.

How do you find a spiritual path? It's a wonderful field to explore: you can meet some extraordinary people, make new friends and learn a lot. Try out some different paths before you make a choice. Start by asking people around you: they may not talk about their beliefs until you ask them. Go to a few services, social events or retreats. Read a few books. You'll find more pointers in Resources.

Choosing a spiritual path is really more a matter of letting it choose you. Try to get your logical mind and your ego out of the way, open up to a sense of where you're drawn to, what inspires you and someone you can learn from. I have had superb individuals as teachers in all the four traditions which are woven into my path.

SUFI WISDOM FOR MATURING MEN

A few men beyond fifty are clearly seeking a spiritual thread to help them find meaning and purpose in life. However, many men of this age just feel lost and confused, even depressed. What's the point of my life? What legacy do I want to leave behind me? These are hard questions and Sufi wisdom may be helpful.

There's no easy definition of Sufis or Sufism. It's certainly not a religion: there are no temples, no one holy book or teacher. Yet a best-selling poet in the UK and US for years has been Rumi, a Sufi poet from the thirteenth century. The quote at the start of the chapter gives you an idea of his approach.

No one is sure how Sufism began: the story I like is that the early Sufis were a mystical Christian group who later adopted the Arabic language and Islamic practices, as Islam swept across the Middle East. If you go back to the source texts in their original language, the beliefs are similar anyway.

One of the first Sufi teachers I met was asked, 'What is Sufism?' He replied, 'It's a way of meeting life from the heart, seeing the divine unity in all beings.' Twenty years later, I'd still call this a good summary. The relevance for men beyond fifty is to stop meeting life from the head, stop trying to understand and control everything, and start treating yourself and all beings with compassion.

A favourite prayer of mine, used by many Sufis, is *ihdina sirat almustaqim*, translated by Neil Douglas-Klotz, a leading Sufi teacher, as:

> *We ask you to reveal our next harmonious steps,*
> *Show us the path that says, 'Stand up, get going, do it!'*
> *That resurrects us from the slumber of the drugged*
> *and leads to consummation of Heart's desire,*
> *like all the stars and galaxies in time, in time, straight on.*
>
> PART OF *SURA FATEHA*,
> TRANSLATED IN *DESERT WISDOM*

While you can get a flavour of the Sufi path by reading poems and websites, to find the real depth you need to spend time face to face with a teacher. Most Sufi orders emphasise the line of personal transmission, from the great Sufi teachers of previous generations, through to the many talented ones of today. If you really want to continue along this path, the best way is usually to commit to a specific teacher and Sufi order and to seek initiation. One of the first initiated Sufis I ever met was also an Anglican vicar, who had his Bishop's permission to be a Sufi too. This is one of the great features of Sufism, that it can weave along with many other spiritual paths.

One of the threads of Sufi wisdom is fellowship with all beings. This can help us feel connected and steady, not lost in a huge universe. Sometimes the image of the Caravan of Creation is used: imagine all humanity like a caravan travelling slowly across the desert. Our ancestors go before us and we receive their legacy, as future generations following behind us will receive what we leave.

The theme of surrendering to a greater power, within yourself and the universe, is a key Sufi teaching. One of my favourite books is *The Last Barrier* by Reshad Feild. It's the story of an Englishman who travels to Turkey, searching for Sufi wisdom, learning that he needs to unlearn and surrender in order to receive. It has the wonderful line, 'Divine guidance is to bring a man to the point of perplexity'. True surrender is nothing to do with despair or abdication: it means knowing your limitations and playing the part in life that's appropriate. Some of the best Sufi teachings come from poets like Rumi or Hafiz.

There is a community of the spirit.
Join it, and feel the delight
of walking in the noisy street
and being the noise.

Drink all your passion,
and be a disgrace.
Close both eyes
to see with the other eye.

FROM *ESSENTIAL RUMI*, BY COLEMAN BARKS

Their poems show how our love for earthly things, especially women, wine and song, express our deeper longing for union with the One, the Beloved. Men beyond fifty can get lost in speculating on their past or their future, so these reminders to take total delight in the present are good for them. So let's end with a song:

We'll drink the wine down to the last
Drink with the Beloved
Take this breath like it's your last
Drink with the Beloved.
We're a caravan you see
Moving towards our destiny
You must find the eyes to see
Drink with the Beloved.

Go to the East, go to the West
Drink with the Beloved
You can't escape this birth and death
Drink with the Beloved.
Watch the drunkards reel and spin
Feel the presence from within
Toasting to the dearest friends
Drink with the Beloved.

FACE YOUR DYING TO ENRICH YOUR LIVING

Do you wonder what's the point of thinking about death? Maybe you're in fine health now, so it seems irrelevant. There's a good reason to consider death now, which is: *you can enrich every day of your life by your awareness of death.*

If you talk to those who work with dying people, or read books like Stephen Levine's, you'll see that many experience dying as a gentle transition, a release. If you find death scary, dig into the reasons: they may just be the general taboo on this topic in our society. If you have real fears, the sooner you can face them the sooner you're free to enjoy life fully. For help with this, see Resources.

> **'I'm not afraid of death: I just don't want to be there when it happens.'**
> *Woody Allen*

Can you say that you have faced up to death, in a practical, emotional and spiritual sense? It's liberating to do so. If you have a partner or adult kids, talk to them about your will and your funeral preferences. This helps to normalise the topic of dying: and if you start with practicalities, it makes it easier for you and those close to you to talk about the feelings too. This section should help you to start engaging with this big topic. Here are some initial pointers:

◆ Look at the animal or plant world – death is a natural part of the cycle. What are your hang-ups about it?

◆ Realise you cannot control the time of your death. Yes, you can take care of your health, but you could be hit by a bus, have a heart attack or be diagnosed with cancer tomorrow. It's better to face the prospect of dying now: this makes it easier when it does happen.

◆ Let go of the illusion that you're in control of your life. In death and life, all you can do is influence, not control, and realising this can bring you to a more realistic two-way relationship with the world around you, and free you from the stress of trying to control everything.

◆ Do Exercises 1 and 2 in Appendix 3. Yes, really: *do them now*. They will truly help you enjoy living to the full and help you clarify what's important in life for you.

◆ If there are things you want to say to people before you die, *do it now*. It can enrich the rest of the time you have with them and ensure that you get the chance to do it.

◆ Cultivate gratitude: appreciation arises naturally when you recognise that this moment is all you have, this life could end any time. Thankfulness will enrich your life and others around you.

◆ Live every day as if it's your last: doing this will help you focus on what matters, drop resentments and petty conflicts and apologise where you need to. At a time when Linda and I had big relationship problems, this one principle transformed the situation.

◆ Get your admin straight – ie will, funeral, papers and financial records.

Life beyond life

What do you believe lies beyond death? Ponder this – take the question into solo time in nature. And ask others what they believe: it can lead to some interesting conversations. If you do believe there is something beyond death – let's call it a life of the spirit – try to contact it now, in this life. If you can live here, with a connection to the life beyond, it can guide and enrich the rest of this lifetime.

I'd like to describe my beliefs about the soul's journey: I'm not asking you to share them, but to show how exploring your beliefs can help you. In Reshad Feild's book *The Last Barrier*, a Sufi teacher says, 'The Soul is a knowing substance. If you know who you are then you know what it is, and that substance permeates all life, but first you must find your soul, your essential self. You must discover who and what you are, and only then will you be at the threshold of the Way.'

I believe we have a soul that travels through numerous lifetimes on its journey, and which chooses each life it comes into, including parents, partners and other major circumstances. This belief means that instead of feeling like a victim about problems in my life, I say that my soul has chosen this situation and I need to find the gift, the growth point in the problem.

At age sixty-three, I did a four-day retreat with Jeremy Thres on Conscious Death and Dying. This was at Hazel Hill Wood and happened while I was writing this chapter. One of the processes we worked on was called a Purpose Circle: this was time alone to take stock of our life, as if we were about to die. For me, a key part of this was to ask my soul for feedback. The response I got was powerful.

> *Soul: You've hardly begun on my hopes for this life. You are not fully within the spiritual life. Your fears of intimacy and of surrender, to the divine and to the feminine, hold you back. The purpose of being in this life is not to take control – that's a self-protective device and an illusion. You have learned most when not in control, even though it's been painful and frightening. Do not retreat from what frightens you: stand fast or move towards it. You can only do this if you entrust yourself to a power greater than you, to the divine.*

Later in the retreat, I imagined myself dying and then experiencing a state beyond death. For me, this is part of the life of the spirit, where the soul travels on without the body. In this state I could meet again dead family or friends, especially my father. Looking back at my life from this stage helped strengthen my intent to follow my soul's advice. I imagined breathing very slowly and deeply as a way to connect myself back to here and now. The result was not a feeling that this world and my work in it are irrelevant, but a shift to a different attitude. As my soul put it:

> *You can include the qualities of the spirit side in your everyday life here – breathe them in through the soul, let them spread through you, especially to the Higher Self. Your work in this life is important, but at the Elder stage is far better done from a centre of surrender and soul than from a need for control.*

Is this where I get off?

So far, this section is mainly aimed at men whose death is years away. With average UK male life expectancy at seventy-seven years, this should fit many of you reading this. However, some of you may be dying now or facing a life-threatening condition such as cancer. Others may have a partner or close friend in this situation. If so, Chapter 5 is relevant for you.

This section is the best help I can offer, accepting that it's very different to be in this for real. A couple of times I've had symptoms which could have been a life-threatening illness, but within a couple of weeks the tests cleared me. I've had several friends with cancer, strokes and other potentially fatal conditions: some have recovered, some have passed on. And I've read the books of Stephen Levine, which share his years of experience with people in this situation. My pointers are these:

- ◆ Facing death or the possibility of death is usually a shipwreck of life as you knew it. You may risk drowning in bewilderment, confusion and fear. Try to find your centre in this moment, in the heart, in choosing to focus on positive qualities like gratitude, trust and love.

- ◆ Stephen Levine comments that patients who meet conditions like cancer by fighting them have more stress and poorer recovery rates than those who meet their health challenge positively, engage with it and learn through it. See his books for more on this.

- ◆ Combine surrender and acceptance that living or dying can be okay for you, with a commitment to do all you can to recover your health and get whatever help you need.

- ◆ A spiritual path, practice and teacher can be of huge help to you now: if you don't have one yet, it's not too late to find one.

- ◆ While this may not seem fair, realise that you may have to give some support to a few of those closest to you. I have seen several couples where the dying person was more calm and centred than their partner.

- ◆ You may find that some of your friends can't cope with your condition: it may trigger their distress about things they can't control, their fear of death and so on. If such friends are a drain on you, ask them to stay away.

- ◆ Look for the joys and good bits, however brief and small: appreciate everything you can.

◆ If you are a partner or friend of someone who is facing death, accept that you cannot magically resolve the situation, but know that your witnessing, your being and feeling with them can help them.

HELLO LANDSCAPE MY OLD FRIEND: NATURE AS GUIDE AND HEALER

Those who contemplate the beauty of the earth find reserves of strength that will endure as long as life lasts.

RACHEL CARSON

Nature is not just landscapes, it's also seas and lakes, the nourishing heat of the sun, the other-worldly glow of the moon, and even the wind and the rain. For many people, nature is a major source of inspiration, and it can also help you to calm down, open up and heal your hurts: all of which leaves you more open to finding vision and purpose.

Men beyond fifty have a deep need for some stability and nurturing, when so much may be changing and falling away from them. Nature can provide this, especially woodlands. So if you make friends with a few landscapes which are special to you, as I have done with Hazel Hill Wood (see next section). Men need to feel okay alone and in the company of other men: special places can help this too: Hazel Hill has hosted many wonderful men's groups. Landscapes really can be like an old friend, with the same sense of recognising familiar features and discovering new ones, plus the reassuring sense that some things are changing only slowly.

If you're wary of anything spiritual and like everything practical and measurable, you risk undervaluing the role that nature can play in your life. In fact, there are research studies showing the measurable benefits on physical, emotional and spiritual wellbeing from time in nature. Here are some of the ways you can achieve these benefits:

◆ Spend at least one hour twice a week walking in nature, and better still, half an hour sitting still and silent (which some would call meditating).

169

◆ If there's an important question in your life that you're perplexed by, stop analysing and fretting about it, take a walk in nature, simply carrying the question and being open to whatever insights you receive.

◆ If you're feeling stressed or tired, spend some time relaxing and picturing yourself feeling happy in a favourite landscape, as a way of resourcing yourself: you can do this anywhere.

◆ Consider spending a longer time out in nature, perhaps in a wood, as a way of finding a vision, or bringing more healing and calm into your life, or doing a wisdom quest: see the later section in this chapter.

◆ Ask a tree! There are many people beside me who believe trees carry special wisdom and healing, which you can access if you are open and patient. For more on this, see the book *Tree Wisdom* in Resources.

HAZEL HILL WOOD: A VERY SPECIAL PLACE FOR MEN

Hazel Hill is a magical seventy-acre wood near Salisbury, which I have owned since 1987. It has been an amazing catalyst for vision, healing and lots more, for me and many other men over the years, so I'd like to share the story with you. This will build on the previous section and show you in more depth how nature can help you on your journey. To get these benefits, you don't need to own a wood: come and enjoy mine!

In 1987, aged thirty-nine, I was still in the thick of my workaholic business career, but knew that I needed to move on, reinvent myself and expand. I had just received a chunk of capital from share options in the business I was running and wondered what I could do with this money that I'd really *enjoy*. Out of nowhere came the idea, *you could buy a wood*. I was inspired by the idea and after a few months of research, bought Hazel Hill.

Since the mid 1990s, Hazel Hill has been a conservation woodland and retreat centre, with lovely wooden eco-buildings, diverse wildlife habitats and a fascinating range of groups using them. However, I didn't start with a vision or a business plan for any of this. I followed a strong inspiration to buy the wood, and everything else has unfolded, slowly and organically, through listening to the wisdom of the wood. The catalyst for all this was vision questing: in 1992, when my kids were entering their teenage years, I wanted to do something to help adolescents approaching adult life. Vision quests are a rite of passage also relevant for maturing men: you can read more about them in the section below.

I started co-leading vision quests for teenagers at Hazel Hill in 1992. These awoke me to the dialogue which I and others could have with the wood, with individual trees, with nature and the spiritual world, so that Hazel Hill is a kind of gateway to these deeper connections. Stewarding this wood has been a profound education in sustainability. For a start, you have to think long-term: in Wiltshire, pine trees take sixty years to mature and prime hardwoods like oak or beech take well over a hundred. Changes happen slowly, and you have to think about posterity: many of the benefits of our current forestry and conservation work will be felt far beyond my lifetime. Secondly, the wooden buildings used by groups are low-impact and mostly off-grid: we have PV electric systems, composting toilets, reed beds for grey water, and visitors have to sort, take away and recycle all their rubbish. When you're at the wood, your impacts on the environment are visible, so it's a great place for learning about sustainable living.

> **'No man manages his affairs as well as a tree does.'**
> *George Bernard Shaw*

The more time you spend in a special landscape and the deeper your relationship, the more it can support you when you need it. When my wife finally called an end to our marriage struggles, I was shattered. It was the wood which gave me the most comforting and parenting through this shipwreck: I recall spending three days there in shock and grief, partly alone, partly with a couple of close friends from my men's group.

If you go into a church or mosque, you feel a special atmosphere: this is a place set apart from everyday life, where generations of people have come to make a spiritual connection. The same is true for landscapes, but in a different way: here, you're open to the sky, the stars, the sun, and direct contact with all the beauty and wisdom of nature. I'd say that Hazel Hill has become a sacred landscape, through twenty years of people being here with this intent. It's worth finding a landscape which feels sacred for you, or creating one.

Here are the main roles which Hazel Hill has played in my journey through the maturing years. I hope you can find places that do the same for you.

One-off men's weekends. I have co-led many weekend workshops and retreats for men at Hazel Hill, and they have been some of the deepest I've experienced. Being out together in a wood gives men a unique sense of fellowship, perhaps recalling our primitive times as hunting bands. There's also a quality of safety, being able to open up and share deeply, which comes from being in a men-only group, out in a sacred landscape. I've seen many men voice painful feelings which they had carried alone for years, finding healing from being witnessed and accepted, not judged, by a company of men. Growing from this comes a stronger, happier sense of self, realising that who you really are is okay.

Solo quests. Hazel Hill has been used by myself and numerous other maturing men, and I highly recommend the wisdom quest for all men beyond fifty. See more in the section below.

Conservation work. Michael Meade, one of the pioneers of men's development in the US, says that men of all ages connect best shoulder to shoulder, not face to face: meaning that when men work together on a physical task, this creates a setting where it's easier for them to open up. The men's groups at the wood usually include conservation projects, and they're a great catalyst.

Seasonal celebrations. The Celtic and many other native traditions celebrate each turn in the year's cycle out on the land. Having organised seasonal celebrations at Hazel Hill for many years, we now have a rolling community of people who come together for a weekend at the eight main festivals: this means the Solstice and Equinox points, and the cross-quarter festivals between them. The wood provides a superb mirror and guide for people, helping them to move through the seasons of their year and their life.

Men and women. Hazel Hill is an important place not only for men, but also for women and for their relationships. The wood enables sharing wisdom between men and women, and exploring sacred relationships. My wife Linda and I initiated our relationship here, and got engaged with a hand-fasting ritual at Hazel Hill.

Ongoing conversation. As well as being at Hazel Hill for many of the groups, I spend a night and day there alone every couple of weeks. This gives me relaxation, renewal, healing and whatever insights I need. As everyday life gets more speedy, complex and technical for most of us, getting back to nature like this becomes more and more crucial.

THE WISDOM QUEST: A RITE OF PASSAGE FOR MATURING MEN

In traditional cultures worldwide, the shift from one life stage to another was marked by rites of passage and ceremonies of initiation for men and women. Two of the most important changes were from child to adult, and from adult to elder. The lack of such rites in Western societies has added to men's confusion about who they are, what their purpose is and how to adapt to major changes. A rite of passage can help you to step out of the previous life stage, and find a fresh sense of self and purpose now. Part of that is seeing how you can serve the wider needs around you. An important part of these rites traditionally is that they would be guided by elders of your own gender, who would help to initiate and welcome you into your new life stage and all that comes with it.

> **'Discontents are often rooted in an unmet longing for wildness, mystery, and a meaningful engagement with the world.'**
> *Bill Plotkin*

The Vision Quest is a classic rite of passage, especially for those entering adulthood, found in native traditions around the world, including Celtic, Norse and Native American. Although details vary, the essence is similar: you spend an extended time alone in one place in nature, for twenty-four to seventy-two hours, usually fasting. Typically, elders will act as guides to prepare you for this time, support you at a distance and welcome you on your return.

Rites of passage for adults becoming elders are more varied and have different names. I'm using the term *Wisdom Quest* for rites of passage which draw from the vision quest tradition, but are tailored to men beyond fifty. The purpose of this section is not to give you a complete guide on how to undertake a Wisdom Quest: I want to show you what one is and how it could help you, so you can decide whether to explore this further.

A central feature of any Vision Quest is that it's a form of death: a stage in your life is gone and needs to be laid to rest, your sense of yourself is dying and has to be reborn. When you're out alone at your chosen spot, through the dark depths of the night, you will be facing your fears, including any fears of death. The preparation for a quest is a bit like preparing to die: handling emotions *and* practicalities, valuing all you have had in your life so far.

The process of a Wisdom Quest begins well before the time out alone, and continues after it. The stages are similar to those of the Hero's Journey, described in Chapter 2, but are often summed up in three stages:

Severance. This first stage should take days or weeks: you are preparing to sever your links with your life to date, to leave everything behind. Part of this process is often an Omen Walk, which helps you recognise issues you need to face in this transition.

Threshold. This is the period of solo time, where you recognise the ending of a part of your life and a part of yourself, where you have the space to meet your fears and find the courage and strength to go beyond them. You have to let go of who you thought you were, to discover a new vision, a new sense of self.

Reincorporation. Similar to the Hero's Return, this is the often difficult stage of bringing your new self and new insights back into the everyday world, fulfilling a new direction, being of service.

While a Wisdom Quest can be carried out alone, I would advise against this, at least for the first time. It's better to have a guide who can support you, teach you and enable you to meet the unexpected. While Vision Quests often use a framework from a specific spiritual tradition, such as Celtic or Native American, you can use this process whatever your beliefs. A Wisdom Quest could use one of these traditions or your own spiritual path. It's a process you can use repeatedly, especially at a major life event: for example, significant birthdays, divorce, death of a parent or loss of a job. Choose your setting carefully: it helps to do your Quest in a sacred landscape where you feel open to the wisdom of nature.

RESOURCES

For these topics, it is best to work with a teacher, group or friend, face to face. Some of these websites can help you to find such contacts, and the books can be a good supplement.

Dreams for awakening

The key to this is your own personal journey, but many of the books below could help.

Memories, Dreams, Reflections, by Carl Jung. ISBN 978-1849028240. This is not a 'how to' book, but it can help you open up to the realms of dreams, the subconscious and the spiritual.

Spiritual dawns

I recommend that you focus on personal contacts and direct experiences rather than books and websites. However, here are a couple you could try:

The Power of Now: A Guide to Spiritual Enlightenment, by Eckhart Tolle. ISBN 978-0340733509. One of the best-selling recent books in this field, and deservedly. Especially helpful for men, since it shows how the mind gets in our way, how to move past this and how to focus on the now.

The Power of Modern Spirituality: How to Live a Life of Compassion and Personal Fulfilment, by William Bloom. ISBN 978-0749952853. I rate William highly as a teacher who is both deep and accessible, and this book has both of these qualities. A good guide to exploring and evolving your own spiritual path, and not linked to any one path or doctrine. Has very good resources for further exploration.

Prayers of the Cosmos, by Neil Douglas-Klotz. ISBN 978-0060619954. If your earlier contact with the Christian faith ended with you dropping out disillusioned, like me, this short and accessible book could help you. It provides extended translations from Aramaic, the language Jesus spoke, which throw a different light on the essential teachings. The book also suggests practices to help you experience and embody these teachings, and it has helped me and others to find a renewed connection with the Christian path.

Desert Wisdom, by Neil Douglas-Klotz. ISBN 978-1456516475. This brilliant book can help you understand and experience some of the deepest teachings from the spiritual traditions of the Middle East, including Sufi, Christian, Islamic and others. It has helped my spiritual path for many years.

Spiritual paths is a topic where web searches are likely to leave you boggled: focusing helps, eg results for 'Celtic spirituality' are less confusing than 'spirituality' in general.

One teacher who I and several friends have found helpful as a starting point is William Bloom (see www.williambloom.com) for his events and publications.

Abwoon Resource Center: This is the website of Neil Douglas-Klotz, a leading international teacher of Sufi, Christian and other Middle Eastern spiritual traditions. The website contains some useful written material, details of all his books and listings of events. See: www.abwoon.com.

There are many different Buddhist orders active in the UK. Here are websites for a couple of them: www.forestsangha.org and www.thebuddhistcentre.com.

Alternatives of St James's Church in London offers a wide variety of evening sessions and longer workshops which can help you experience and explore different paths and teachers. See more at www.alternatives.org.uk.

Facing your dying

Who Dies? An Investigation of Conscious Living and Conscious Dying, by Stephen Levine. ISBN 978-0385262217. A beautifully written book which can help you live well and die well. Much of it is relevant at any time in the mature years, and some is specifically about the time of physical death. There are some good, guided meditations, exploration of what lies beyond death, and useful lists of books and music.

Healing into Life and Death, by Stephen Levine. ISBN 978-0946551484. This excellent book differs from *Who Dies?* (above) in its strong focus on self-healing, with more of a workbook flavour, guided meditations and exercises.

The Tibetan Book of Living and Dying, by Sogyal Rinpoche. ISBN 978-1846041051. Written by one of the most warm and engaging Tibetan Buddhist teachers, this is a relatively approachable way into the deep and complex Tibetan teachings about conscious dying, the life beyond, and how this can enrich life now.

Dying Into Love: This website offers some powerful wisdom from teachers with a lot of experience in this area, such as Ram Dass and Joan Halifax. See: www.dyingintolove.com

Dying Matters: A UK website raising awareness of dying, death and bereavement. It encourages people to talk about dying, and offers useful advice, contacts for support and links to other useful organisations. See: www.dyingmatters.org.

Die-a-log forum: This offers compassionate conversations about death and dying via a growing network of Live Groups, a website with a members-only forum, and open access areas for resources and essential information about death and dying. Set up by Max Mackay-James. See: www.diealog.co.uk.

Sufi wisdom

The Sufis, by Idries Shah. ISBN 978-0863040740. There are various introductions to Sufism: I recommend this one because it is not a mere tour guide or description from the outside. This is written from the inside, by a man immersed in the tradition, and it offers you the chance to experience, not just observe.

The Sufi Book of Life, by Neil Douglas-Klotz. ISBN 978-0142196359. This is a useful book for those starting to explore the Sufi tradition, with a helpful introduction and a list of twelve organisations you could contact about Sufi teachings: not all of these are active in the UK. The main part of the book includes teaching stories and meditations so that you can start to experience some of this for yourself.

The Last Barrier, by Reshad Feild. ISBN 978-0060625863. As mentioned earlier, this is the story of one man's search for Sufi wisdom. Beautiful, moving and a powerful way of conveying the nature of the Sufi path.

The Essential Rumi, translated by Coleman Barks. ISBN 978-0965064873. This is one of the best collections, by one of the best translators, and there are many of both. It has some helpful commentary and is delightfully organised, with sections like On Bewilderment, On Spring Giddiness and On Being a Lover.

If you want to make contact with Sufi teachers and experience Sufi practices, it is best to get in touch with one of the various Sufi orders. Some of these, like the two for which websites are given below, are more Western-oriented and are quite active in the UK. Others are more Eastern, more focussed on Islamic practices and may be harder to access.

Sufi Ruhaniat International: The website contains masses of teachings, access to books and CDs and a calendar of events in various countries. See: www.ruhaniat.org.

The Sufi Order: The website contains a range of teachings and contacts for a number of local groups around the UK. See: www.sufiorderuk.org.

Philip O'Donohoe: Philip is one of the most accessible Sufi teachers active in the UK, and several of his events would be a good initial experience of Sufi teachings. See: www.philipodonohoe.co.uk.

Nature as guide and healer

Tree Wisdom, by Jacqueline Memory Paterson. ISBN 978-0722534083. This beautifully written book will help you understand the ways that people for many generations have engaged with trees: for healing, inspiration and other purposes. It has a section on each native British hardwood tree, showing how you can work with it in these ways and its role in folk tradition.

Glennie Kindred: Glennie has deep knowledge of native British plants and trees, and has been leading celebrations of the Celtic festivals and other ceremonies on the land for many years. Her website includes some excellent articles and information about her books, which she has beautifully illustrated: these include *Sacred Celebrations,* which offers traditional and new ways to celebrate the Celtic festivals. See: www.glenniekindred.co.uk.

Hazel Hill Wood

For more information on Hazel Hill Wood, including open events, see www.hazelhill.org.uk. The programme includes men's weekends, conservation groups and seasonal celebrations.

Wisdom quest

The Book of the Vision Quest, by Steven Foster with Meredith Little. ISBN 978-0671761899. A beautifully written book by two of the main teachers who have brought the vision quest tradition to a wider audience. It can help you to understand and explore the idea of calling for a dream.

Finding someone to guide you on a wisdom quest may be complex. A web search can leave you pretty confused. In choosing a guide, ask around, check their website and credentials, and talk to them in person. One network I can recommend, which has clear standards of ethics, but only a few members in the UK, is www.wildernessguidescouncil.org.

Chapter 9

Giving and receiving:
Friends, groups and communities

Learn to remember you got great friends, don't forget that and they will always care for you no matter what. Always remember to smile and look up at what you got in life.

MARILYN MONROE

The midlife years are sometimes called a second adolescence, and this may clarify why friends and groups are so important for men beyond fifty. Remember your own teenage years, or look at the youth today: having a best friend, losing him, feeling part of a peer group or falling out with one, are all hugely important. Teenagers, like maturing men, are in a time of great change, feeling unsure who they are, needing people close to them for reassurance and even for their sense of identity.

It's clear during adolescence that most boys lack the social skills they need, and this remains generally true as the decades roll by. In the fifties and beyond, men's connections with wives, kids and work colleagues are loosening: they need new friends, but often lack the skills to find them. This chapter builds on the previous two: your prospects of making good friends improve as you clear your shadow stuff, break out of destructive habits and find a vision of who you want to be. Shaping yourself from the views of your friends is unwise: better to find friends who support the choices you've made.

This chapter offers guidance on the basic social skills of friendship: how to start them, sustain them and handle conflicts. Then we explore the many forms and functions of groups, the skills you need and the mysteries of group dynamics. Next we consider men's groups: the what, why and how. Then we explore intentional communities, which can vary hugely, but offer a lot of learning and richness.

Are you a giver, taker or receiver? Many men are stuck in one of these roles, but you need to balance all three. Givers (often martyrs) exhaust themselves looking out for others, secretly hoping they'll receive in return. Takers will grab, demand and fight for what they want: sometimes necessary, but often not. Receiving can be hard for men: letting in the things you need and trusting without control.

Give yourself a helicopter view of your patterns and habits with friends. Which of these three roles do you play? Can you see other habits: do you make new connections easily or stick with a few long-term ones? Do you fall out with friends and groups or lose interest quickly? Do you feel unheard, left on the margins? If you don't like what you see, set your intention to change it. Look back at Chapter 2: maybe you're repeating a negative story like rejection in your friendships and group roles. Perhaps you resist going deeper because you lack the social skills or you fear you'll be rejected when you show the real you. Friendship and groups can be as challenging as your main relationship, and they actually need some of the same skills. So it's worth revisiting Communication Skills in Chapter 3.

FRIENDS: OILING THE GEARBOX, TOPPING THE CAKE

One of the big improvements in my life from the thirties and forties to my fifties and sixties has been more and better friendships. I feel very fortunate to have a few deep friendships, plus a lot of pretty good ones: most with men, but a few with women. These friendships oil the gearbox of life: lubricating changes, conflicts and crises which could otherwise be overwhelming. They also top the cake, through the pleasures of companionship, and by witnessing and appreciating good things about me which I often ignore. This may sound easy, but it hasn't been for me. I've had to learn by mistakes and the painful loss of some good friendships.

Looking back at my thirties and forties, I see how awkward I was to be friends with: so uptight, oversensitive, unsure of myself, self-centred, controlling... It has taken a lot of change, both deliberate and unplanned, to improve things: men's groups, co-counselling, divorce and lost friendships have all helped. Like me, you may know men who seem naturally sociable and always have plenty of friends. This section is not for them, but for anyone who needs to work at this, especially men who suffer from shyness, depression or other problems with self-confidence. Even small rebuffs can hurt like hell. Think of this like a child learning to walk: a few tumbles and bruises are only natural. And if you're struggling to find the motivation, remember that the skills you learn in friendship will help you in other arenas, like romance and work. Here are my top tips on cultivating friendship.

◆ Be willing to experiment: trying a range of approaches with a variety of people increases your chances of success.

◆ Realise that there are many kinds of friendships. Be aware of the various kinds you would like and try to sense early on what your potential friend wants. For example, the level of openness and emotional sharing may vary hugely. In many male friendships, all this is unspoken: remember *Last of the Summer Wine*.

◆ Imagine a new friendship as a spiral process: don't plunge in, but let it deepen gradually. Listen for clues from your friend about the subjects they do and don't want to talk about, and guide them on your preferences.

◆ Cultivate your listening skills: try to hear what your friend is saying and *respond* to it. Don't get preoccupied with your own nerves and needs. Listen for what's not being said: many men struggle to express their feelings or ask for support, so listen for clues and make an offer, for example, 'Would it help you to talk more about the divorce?'

◆ Co-counselling training can help with friendship skills, including negotiating contracts. This may sound formal, but it's simply about getting clear expectations between you. Men often share a problem with a friend because they want practical advice, but sometimes they just need a sympathetic ear. Checking what your friend would like from you shows that you care about their needs.

◆ Find the courage to make the first move. In shifting from casual contact towards friendship, someone needs to take the initiative: remember the other guy may be even more shy than you are.

◆ For men, doing something together can be an easier start to a friendship than sitting and talking. It could be quite simple, like going to the cinema or having a walk.

◆ Remember the question early in this chapter about the giver, taker and receiver roles: do you and your friend have a balance between these? If you're stuck in one role, experiment with changing.

◆ As a friendship starts to build, if you want it to deepen, try talking openly with your friend about how it's going and what you both want from it. This kind of frankness doesn't come easy in our culture, but it can help both of you to get what you need and to learn as you go along.

◆ Conflicts between male friends can be quite sudden and severe at any age. Often men lack the skill to express and hear difficult feelings or to use the techniques of conflict resolution. Men may find it easier to dump the friendship than face the conflict. There are some good methods of conflict resolution, such as Non-Violent Communication, which are relevant for friends, groups or communities.

◆ As you change, the kind of friends you want will change too. If you want to move from friendship down to acquaintance, do it honestly: talk it through with your friend, hear their feelings, try to reach a point of completion and celebration for the friendship. This will cause less pain than just stopping.

THE AGE OF GROUPS

Groups come in so many different forms that it's hard to generalise, but this section will have a go. Taking an overview, you could say that most men in their thirties and forties focus on their individual path. In the fifties and beyond, there's a new interest in groups, for a range of reasons. In traditional societies, the role of the elder was often a collective one: groups of elders found wisdom and faced change together. Secondly, as chunks of your life fall away, the wisdom and friendship of groups can help you. Thirdly, many of the crises of our time are so severe that they need group action to resolve them: this is explored more below. Let's look at the kinds of groups we're exploring:

◆ Short-term groups: a business meeting, a conservation work party or an outing to a football match all call for a range of group skills.

◆ Long-term groups go through distinct life cycles (see more below) and can have many purposes, including work, social, learning, healing and spiritual practice.

◆ We now have rapid growth in virtual groups: ongoing ones like forums and chat rooms can still require group skills, and short-term groups such as crowdsourcing can have remarkable power.

◆ Men's groups are a key kind of group for this book and have a separate section below.

◆ While many groups are a kind of community, intentional communities can be especially relevant for maturing men and also have a separate section below.

Take yourself back to your early experiences of groups: in your teenage years and twenties, at school, college, work and social groups. Was there a role you repeatedly played: maybe the joker, the outsider, the leader, the daredevil, the brains? Did you have any idea of what was really going on? All this is relevant to your maturing years, because the roles you played then, and the good or bad experiences you had, will shape your relationship to groups now.

Group dynamics

In recent decades, there has been more understanding of what is often called group dynamics: much of this learning has come from the business sector, some from sociology, but it's relevant to groups of all kinds. Group dynamics include the ways group members interact and the roles they play. My own experience of groups through my teenage years and into my twenties was mostly bewildering and painful. I was often the loner, I couldn't figure out the dynamics, and I was baffled by the people who seemed to shine and succeed.

> **Two's company, but three's a group.**

One of the most widely known, useful and simple models of group dynamics is the four-stage life cycle first defined by Bruce Tuckman:

Forming. In this initial stage, people are getting to know each other and gather impressions about the task. Conflict is avoided as group members are keen to be accepted. Most individuals are focused on themselves as there's not yet much sense of the group. The tasks are still poorly understood, so there's a need for directive leadership.

Storming. This could be called a stage of necessary conflict. There may be debate about what the real objectives are, the priority tasks and who does what. Differing values and priorities may need to be faced and integrated. With good processes and conflict resolution skills, this stage can be relatively quick and productive, but it's often long and painful.

Norming. The group finds consensus about priorities, roles and how to achieve them. This may require compromise, and accepting that some differences of opinion and values can't be resolved and have to be lived with.

Performing. Not all groups reach this point! Good teams can get the job done effectively with little external supervision, handle conflicts and reach good decisions. This usually means that the group has found ways to accept and live with differences among group members.

Groups may go around this cycle repeatedly as new members join or major challenges have to be faced.

Do you recall your answer to the question about the role you played in groups when you were younger? Are you still playing the same role? Learning to play a different role, or moving between several, could be a valuable part of your reinvention in this life stage. Experiment; if you make a few mistakes, you can hopefully learn from them. The Belbin model of the different roles that work groups need in order to function effectively may offer you some new insights and ideas about ways you could contribute differently. You can find more about this in Resources.

Some of the skills which will help you in friendships will also be useful in groups, such as listening, expressing your own needs clearly and handling conflict. However, in many groups you also need great skills in reading between the lines. Criticism and praise may be given very indirectly, and few groups spend the time they need on reviewing and improving their own processes. As one individual, you can usually do no more than give the occasional nudge.

If you feel that major improvement is needed, a solo tirade rarely gets results. Better to build support slowly with others in the group, asking objective questions like *Could we be doing this better?* This is more fruitful than criticising difficult individuals. Having an external coach or facilitator run a team-building session or a health check on the way the group is working can be an effective way to improve its performance. Getting an outsider to provide a safe space where everyone can speak is easier than a member of the group trying to guide the process *and* take part in it. The process of someone leaving a group is often handled poorly. Ideally, the others need to acknowledge the leaver's contributions, celebrate them and even grieve their going. Often people are too embarrassed to do this. And sometimes the leaver prefers to badmouth the group as a way of easing their departure.

MEN'S GROUPS: WHAT, WHY, HOW?

There are many kinds of men's groups, but I'm using the term here to mean an ongoing circle of men who meet regularly with a shared aim of support, wisdom or something similar. Finding these groups is hard: they're not secret, but they have no desire or reason to be publicly visible. Few have a website and many are closed to new members: not for exclusivity, but because they're happy with the group size and the depth you get from a steady membership.

If you want to find a men's group to join, start asking friends. You could also try local counsellors and therapists. You may find a group that's closed to new members: ask if they can set up a waiting list or if there's an open session you could attend. Once the current group have met you, they may even change their policy and expand the circle a bit. Alternatively, consider starting a new men's group: you'll probably find there's plenty of demand.

So what does a men's group do? How is it organised? There's no one answer, but here are some pointers:

Aims. Some groups will have specific, stated aims, others are entirely informal and guided by the needs of the moment.

Organisation. Most men's groups are peer-led, so different members take a lead for different sessions, themes or functions (like venues or new members). Or it can mean that there's a leadership vacuum (see more below). Some groups have one or two men as ongoing leaders and occasionally a professional counsellor who is paid for this work.

Format. Most often, groups will meet for an evening, every two to six weeks. Sometimes they may have longer gatherings. A few ongoing groups meet for one or a few weekends per year.

Support/Challenge. This spectrum is a key zone of debate in many men's groups. Unless the upfront aims are very clear, there can be tension between those who just want to hang out and do a bit of sharing and those who want more intensity, more active processes akin to a therapy group. The group I co-founded in 1992, which still meets every three weeks, has this debate periodically: our best answer is to agree themes and leaders for some sessions and let others share.

Leadership. Whatever the format, this can be a sticky issue. Men's conditioning is to compete with each other, and they can easily resent and resist anyone trying to lead the group, and even isolate them. There are no easy solutions, but making the issue visible, discussing it honestly and deepening trust can all help. So can a periodic session with an outside facilitator who enables the group to face such questions more directly.

Processes. These can vary a lot. One of the commonest is a sharing round, where each man speaks (sometimes with a time limit) about whatever is important for him in this moment, without interruptions or responses from the others. If you're thinking of starting a group, it's well worth doing the Co-counselling Fundamentals training. Members with co-counselling training or professional therapy skills can deepen the capacity of the group.

Group size. A group of six to ten men is big enough to have a collective character, and small enough to feel safe and give everyone a hearing. Allowing for absences, this might imply eight to twelve members. It's possible to function with groups bigger or smaller than this, but many men have found this group size ideal.

Rituals. Rituals here means things that you do in a group, often at the start or end, to increase trust and safety, and make group space different from the everyday. Some men's groups have no ritual, some have elaborate ones, and some may share a spiritual path and use rituals or prayers from that. In my ongoing men's group, we always start and finish by joining hands in the circle and having a couple of minutes' silence.

Starting a men's group?

Starting from scratch can be a good adventure: I've done it twice. But there are a couple of catch-22 problems. Firstly, forming a group requires you to offer some leadership and structure, but if you're aiming for a peer group, potential members may resist this. Secondly, it's only when a group gathers that you discover where the consensus lies for the kind of group it could be and can see if all the individuals fit. You may find yourself in the awkward position of initiating a group whose preferred direction is not yours or wondering how to ease out men whose approach disrupts the original aims.

One helpful strategy is to co-found a group with one or two other men. This reduces the risk of a one-versus-the-rest situation and it's easier for co-leaders to take a stand on awkward issues if that's needed. When a group starts, have three or four trial meetings, where you get to know each other, build up trust and experiment with approaches, before trying to define what kind of group you want and who will be in it. If you have divergences about basic aims, eg challenge versus support, be willing to face a split in the group, and maybe the creation of two new groups: it's better than fudging the issue and continuing with a basic conflict inside the group.

As the group starts to develop, agree norms, for example confidentiality and not interrupting others. Don't get too upset if members leave in the early months. This is a new experience for many men and this may feel too challenging or exposing. And if it really does run out of steam, wind it up with gratitude as a good learning experience.

COMMUNITIES: WHAT'S IN IT FOR YOU?

Communities is another term with a wide range of meanings. Your local neighbourhood may be a community in some sense, or your Twelve Step group, or your cricket club. However, I want to focus on intentional communities: this means groups of people living and often working with a shared set of aims and values. Even these can take many forms: here are some of the most common:

◆ *Ecological groups*. You can live more lightly on the earth by sharing resources with others, and a growing number of projects have this aim: ranging from a couple of benders (canvas structures with wood-burning stoves) to full-blown ecovillages.

◆ *Spiritual communities*. Most often, these are focused on a specific teacher or doctrine, such as Holy Isle in Scotland, a

Tibetan Buddhist centre.

◆ *Cohousing neighbourhoods.* These combine self-contained
living spaces with shared facilities, such as a large room
for group meals and parties, a kids' playroom, maybe a
community market garden.

◆ *Communes.* Many people believe all communities are
communes, but they're not! A commune has limited private
space (maybe just bedrooms), so meals and social spaces
are shared. They may have a strong political slant, or income
sharing, or a sustainability goal.

◆ *Ecovillages.* These are important pioneering centres, but
there are few real ecovillages in the UK. I can recommend
the Findhorn Foundation in Scotland as a genuine ecovillage and a spiritual community.

Most communities get lots of one-off visitors, so don't expect
to get the full flavour of a place or the people on a first drop-
in. If you visit regularly, maybe as a volunteer helper or taking
part in workshops, you will start to feel part of the community.
However, if you want to be fully part of it, with both the benefits and stresses that brings, you need to live there. At least go for
a few weeks. You may want to consider joining for six months
or indefinitely: it works well for some maturing men.

What's in it for me?

This is a trick question! If you hope a community will magically
meet your needs – heal your neuroses, cure your loneliness or
dish up a super partner – revise your expectations. I've seen a lot
of people who seek out community thinking it will take care of
everything: it doesn't.

Community can bring you growth and happiness, but it's
often a tough road. You must take responsibility for yourself
and be willing to give before you receive. If you feel needy and
depleted, find other ways to heal and resource yourself. And

here's another warning: communities can be demanding on you in time and money. The workload usually exceeds capacity: there's always more to do, plus all those meetings. As for money: in some communities you pay even to visit, while others give you pocket money for working. Regard it as an investment!

So with all these warnings, what *is* in it for you? Why take this path? I lived in a cohousing community for five years, and have stayed in many others. Here are some of the potential benefits:

Personal growth. You can be pretty sure that a community will speed up your learning about yourself, perhaps in challenging ways. There's more intensity, more mirroring, more direct communication and, – if you're lucky – more support to help you in your journey.

Social skills. While the quality of social skills may vary hugely, you should find some people who are role models and some good group processes, so it's a useful place to learn.

Work skills. Communities have an endless need for labour, so it's a great way to try things and gather skills: especially manual skills like gardening, building or cooking, but maybe others like education or group facilitation.

Service. Many communities aim to live and teach something valuable, such as sustainability or spirituality. If you want to be of service, this can be a powerful place to do so.

How do I apply?

Probably another trick question. Getting involved with a community or even just visiting can be a slow and messy process. They can be slow at answering emails and hard to reach by phone. If you want to explore intentional communities, here are my tips:

◆ *Do some background reading.* The first two books in the Communities section of Resources can give you a flavour of this sector and how to approach it.

◆ *Brush up your interpersonal skills.* Use some of the Resources in this chapter and Chapter 3. For example, do a training course in co-counselling or Non-Violent Communication. It will help you and show communities that you're serious.

◆ *Set your goals.* Try to clarify the *kind* of community you'd like to find, how you would assess it and what you can offer them. The good ones get lots of approaches: why should they let *you* in?

◆ *Preliminary research.* Use directories, web searches and phone calls to get a feel for suitable projects, and make a shortlist of those that interest you most.

◆ *Initial visits.* You could make these anything from a few hours to a week. Try to find ways of getting involved, not just drifting around. Helping with work tasks and cooking is a good move. Scan the notice boards, observe how residents relate with each other. Understand how money works. If you stay for a few days, ask for feedback: how do they rate your skills and potential for the community?

◆ *Consider a longer commitment.* If you've found somewhere you feel drawn to, consider what your goals would be for a longer visit. Can you balance this with other commitments, such as a partner or ageing parents? Can you fit the community's needs and structures? By this stage, most groups should agree to meet you to discuss all this before you commit.

RESOURCES

See the Communication skills and assertiveness section of Chapter 3 Resources for skills which will help with all aspects of this chapter.

Friends

How to Start a Conversation and Make Friends, by Don Gabor. ISBN 978-1451610994. If you're lacking confidence about this topic, this is short, basic, friendly and sensible.

Social Intelligence, by Daniel Goleman. ISBN 978-0099464921. A great book for those who want analytical, scientific explanations for the world of feelings and human relations. Relevant for friendships, group dynamics and working relationships. Draws on such fields as neuro-sociology, biology and brain science, but in a way which some men (including me) will find readable and helpful.

www.succeedsocially.com: A helpful, clear, extensive website with good basic advice, plus specific help on issues like shyness.

If you're unsure where to look for potential friends, use the internet to find local groups for something that interests you. Activities such as conservation, sports or hobbies are especially good ways for men to get to know each other.

Men's Sheds Network: There is a growing network of Men's Sheds in the UK: these are places to make informal friendships while sharing practical skills such as woodworking. The website also offers advice on how to start your own Shed group. See: www.menssheds.org.uk.

Groups

It's hard to find a simple book about the everyday skills of being part of a group. While the first two books below focus on leading groups, they are short, straightforward and useful for group members too.

Facilitating Groups, by Jenny Rogers. ISBN 978-0335240968. Includes a good chapter on dynamics of groups, useful bits about group skills and a lot about facilitation.

The Red Book of Groups, by Gaie Houston. ISBN 978-0951032336. This delightfully quirky book dates from 1990, but is available used. It has good basic sections about different kinds of groups, processes and troubleshooting.

The Different Drum, by M. Scott Peck. ISBN 978-0099780304. A passionate book about the power of groups where there is enough trust to share deeply and support each other. Good for men's groups, spiritual and support groups.

Group Dynamics and Community Building: If you search the 'group dynamics' section of this website, you will find a large range of processes and insights about how groups work and how to help them work better. It is more aimed at community or social groups, and includes stories and poems which can help build trust and cooperation. See: www.community4me.com.

Free Management Library: Although this has a business focus, the group dynamics section has some useful material, including the forming-storming-norming-performing model. See: www.managementhelp.org.

Belbin: Includes descriptions of the Nine Team Roles. See: www.belbin.com.

Men's groups

Finding an existing men's group to join is difficult, since most of them have no website or other public visibility. You could try the UK Men for Change Network: this has a list of contact people around the UK and also offers a service where men looking to join or create a group can put the word out. The Network has a freespace website – do a web search for 'UK Men for Change Network' and you should find it. UK Men for Change also has a useful listing of national men's work groups, websites and events, but some of its listings may be out of date.

Network for Men and Boys: This is a new website which aims to create a listing for all types of organisations working with men or boys in the UK, hopefully including local men's groups. See: www.nfmb.org.uk.

Men Beyond 50: One aim of the Men Beyond 50 Network, both co-founded by Alan Hecks and Max Mackay-James, is to help maturing men make local contacts and form or join a local ongoing men's group. See: www.menbeyond50.net.

ManKind Project: This is a relatively large network of men in the UK, Ireland, USA and many other countries. There are also Elders Circles within MKP. Once you've done their initiatory weekend, The Adventure, you can join a local ongoing group. I know several men who have tried MKP: it has been good for most, but not all. The website has advice about checking it out first, which I suggest you do. See: www.uk.mkp.org.

If you do a web search on 'men's groups UK', you will find a number of specific groups listed: many are faith groups or gay groups, and a few are run by a professional facilitator and require payment.

A Gathering of Men: The Story of Creating a Men's Group to Address Perennial Male Issues, by Derek Stedman. ISBN 978-0595408658. Amazingly, there are almost no books about starting or running a men's group. This is an American book about a group of men in their fifties and sixties, which interweaves quite a lot of anecdote with some good practical advice.

Talking with our Brothers, by George Taylor. ISBN 978-0964412903. This 1996 book is a good guide to starting and running a men's group, with a range of useful, detailed processes. However, it is now difficult and expensive to buy.

Menweb: Includes a range of useful articles and processes for men's groups, some being excerpts from George Taylor's book. See: www.menweb.org.

Menletter: If you want a really basic two page brief on starting a group, this is it! See: www.menletter.org.

Communities

Cohousing in Britain: A Diggers & Dreamers Review, edited by Sarah Bunker, Chris Coates, Martin Field and Jonathan How. ISBN 978-0954575731. A good overview, including general principles plus case studies on actual projects.

Diggers and Dreamers, by Sarah Bunker, Chris Coates and Jonathan How. ISBN 978-0954575724. For many years this has been the leading guide to intentional communities in the UK. The articles at the front offer helpful briefing too.

Creating a Life Together: Practical Tools to Grow Ecovillages and Intentional Communities, by Diane Leafe Christian. ISBN 978-0865714717. This is my favourite 'how to' book in this field, by an American who lives in an ecovillage and edited *Communities Magazine* in the US. Has great sections like 'The Successful Ten Per Cent – and Why Ninety Per Cent Fail'. Strikes a good balance between the human dynamics and the structural/logistical issues, which are both crucial.

Diggers & Dreamers: Masses of useful material, including books about community living published by Diggers & Dreamers, articles and links, also an online directory to many UK communities and a notice board section where you could announce your interest in finding other people to start a group. See: www.diggersanddreamers.org.uk.

UK Cohousing Network: Includes useful general briefing and a directory (not comprehensive) of both established and forming cohousing groups, plus a range of resources. See: www.cohousing.org.uk.

Chapter 10

Sex: The best years, no kidding!

It's absolutely unfair for women to say that guys only want one thing: sex. We also want food.

JAROD KINTZ

The years beyond fifty could well be the best sexual times of your life. This is not vague optimism: I've done many tantra groups and have heard many couples in their fifties, sixties and seventies sharing how good it is and how they got there. However, it's no good treating sex like sanitation: something you hope happens of its own accord, because it creates a stink if it goes wrong. Sex is another part of your life which will need reinvention, a willingness to learn and change. And it will need this from you and your partner. For a start, you need to learn how to talk about sex: with your partner, with men you can learn from and maybe a good teacher.

I've spent a lot of time in groups of men over fifty: the topic of sex is rarely discussed. Do you think that's because everything's okay? I believe it's because we're off the map without a compass. We have no idea what's normal any more and we dare not share our problems for fear of shame and ridicule: 'Hey guys, this fellow actually can't...' Locker-room mockery still haunts us and here again is the second adolescence. When you can create the safety and permission for maturing men to talk about sex, the doubts and vulnerability are very moving. So I hope that this chapter and its resources will give you clarity, confidence and years of sexual delight.

We'll start with what's changing in physiology for men in their fifties, sixties and beyond: you're not imagining it, you're not alone, there *are* big shifts going on. Then we explore how sex and relationship fit, and how to make these the best sexual years of your life, including the delights of slow sex. Next we explore what tantra is really about, and finally we visit the female menopause. There's a fair chance that your partner is pre-, post- or full-on menopause, and if so, you can't ignore it.

A good sexual relationship is an art: it can't be learned mechanically. But like handling emotions, there's a lot of skills and knowledge which can help you. It's worth investing time and money in this, and it can be some of the most fun you've ever had while learning.

Sexual problems are ultra painful. For one thing, you can't hide them, it's right there between you and your partner. For another, sex defies men's desire to treat every problem like a wonky car and fix it mechanically. As someone said, 'In sleep, sex and fishing, the more you try, the less happens'. Having had an averagely good sex life in my thirties and forties, the years since then have seen some humiliating failures, the realisation I had lots to learn, and some ecstatic sex beyond my fantasies. You won't find this on the High Street, but there's a lot of expertise and a few good teachers out there who can help you.

> **'The difference between sex and death is, with death you can do it alone and nobody's going to make fun of you.'**
> *Woody Allen*

Problems in most parts of your life will impact in your sexual experiences. It's sad but true that feelings like low self-confidence or depression do lower the libido, so you risk a vicious spiral of feeling that nothing's going right. However, the good news is that most women don't expect men to *perform* 24/7: if you can stop judging yourself, you'll probably find her really understanding. And the other good news is that as you sort out other problems, such as anger, anxiety or addiction, it can really benefit your sex life.

SEX FOR MEN BEYOND FIFTY: THE SOFT FACTS

Sex for maturing men won't be business as usual. It changes for all of us, but you can choose to see the gifts in the changes. One big reason for the difference is that testosterone levels decline from the age of forty. Another is that nerve functions become less responsive. And most physical or emotional health problems, such as high blood pressure, heavy drinking or depression will affect your sex life more as you grow older.

What does this mean in practice? Firstly, it takes longer to get an erection, and it may depend more on physical stimulation and less on erotic imaginings. Secondly, erections are typically less firm and shorter in duration. Thirdly, the nature of orgasm changes: the muscular contractions are less intense, ejaculation is slower and semen volume is lower.

None of this needs to depress you, unless you still aspire to the sexual performance of a sports jock in his twenties. However, it's likely that your partner is maturing too, and that she's not after a three-minute jocking. In fact, all of the changes above can be turned to advantage.

A write-up from Harvard Health Publications delightfully explains that an erection is both a hydraulic event (requiring a six-fold increase in the amount of blood in the penis) and a chemical event. The fairly recent discovery of the chemical aspect has led to medications like Viagra. If you want to pursue that route, do a web search for comments from users and their partners. I have not used Viagra, and don't intend to, as I feel it puts the focus on penetrative, genital sex, and not the relationship. If you want more frequent or durable erections, there are other ways to do this, such as diet, exercise and herbal supplements. See more in Resources.

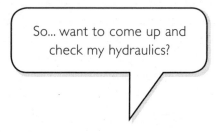

A common teaching in Taoist and other Eastern approaches to sexuality is semen retention, ie the benefits to men of refraining from ejaculation. These benefits can include higher levels of energy, testosterone and libido: especially valuable for older men, and Taoist sexual teachers advocate that the frequency of ejaculation should reduce with age: for example once a week in the sixties, once a month in the seventies. I have found that this fits well with maturing sexuality, but it needs to be approached with care. It's best to explore this with guidance and supervision from a Taoist, Tantra or other suitable teacher.

HAND IN GLOVE: SEX AND RELATIONSHIP

If your sex life is poor, you may be tempted to try something different: maybe threesomes, one-night stands, affairs, bondage or recreational drugs. Some men try these when they're out of relationship, some alongside it and some with their partner. I'm sorry to sound dull, but my advice is, don't go that way. If your sex life needs improving, technique may help, but the biggest place to look is the relationship itself. In my life and for many other men, I've seen how relationships and sex mirror each other with ruthless accuracy.

If there are feelings not voiced or not faced between you and your partner it will show in the sexual connection. You may both settle for excuses and patience when the sex isn't good, but if you look truthfully at how things have been for the past few weeks, what's really going on? As the song says, *'When love goes wrong, nothing goes right'*.

So what's to be done? Go back to Chapter 3 on relationships and take stock. Treat sexual problems as a call for you and your partner to take the risk of deeper truth. For many men, honesty with a partner about difficult emotions or sexual problems is not easy. However, realising that the sexual issues reflect the emotional ones may help you, and most women will value more emotional openness and vulnerability from their partner.

At the root of many relationship and sexual problems is what I call terror of intimacy. Take some time alone and imagine being totally intimate with your partner, your innermost self revealed, naked, to its deepest place: how does this feel? For many men, this depth of intimacy feels unbearably painful: it reconnects them with the worst pain of their childhood, which is what hides in the depths. It brings up terror that your partner will reject you when she finally gets to see your innermost reality. You can increase the intimacy between you by steadily building up the trust, by each giving loving parenting to the hurt child in the other, by pursuing your own healing path and getting support as a couple if you need it.

> **If we didn't have something to hide,**
> **we wouldn't be human...**

As well as the deep wounds, another barrier to intimacy is the negative emotions and patterns which can become habits for a couple. My favourite book on relationships, *Getting the Love you Want* (see Chapter 3 Resources) can help shift these patterns and is great for men, because it provides a very clear structure of actions which bring positive emotional change. Its ten-step process is designed to deepen love, and will lead to a sweeter, deeper sexual relationship too.

One of the gifts of sexual problems now is showing what you need to heal from your past. Maybe you have felt like a sexual failure in previous relationships, or perhaps your sexual self-confidence was hammered in your teenage or early adult years. If you suffered sexual or other abuse in childhood, it can create lasting damage to your willingness to trust and open up to others. There are good books, therapists and support organisations that can help with all these and other sexual issues. It's worth facing such challenges now, because the more you do so, the better the partner you'll be ready for.

IT'S IN FRONT OF YOU! THE BEST SEXUAL YEARS OF YOUR LIFE

> *In the twilight he stands, an elder,*
> *his heart in his hands.*
> *His body, dignified or droopy:*
> *It's all in the eye of the beholder.*

Joel Block is an American psychologist specialising in couples and sexuality, who supports my optimism. Here's an excerpt from his book:

Couples at fifty are on the threshold of a richer, fuller, and more mature sex life than they have enjoyed in the past. Adults-only sex not only can but will be emotionally satisfying and thrilling physically. Although physiological changes dictate that we make certain adaptations to our lovemaking styles, we are also the beneficiaries of some potent sexual benefits at midlife. They include:

◆ *Greater sophistication about our own and our partner's sexuality*

◆ *Increased capability of communicating our sexual and emotional needs without fear of looking silly or being rejected or misunderstood by the one we love*

◆ *Improved sexual responsiveness in women and a corresponding improved ability to control ejaculation in men*

◆ *Greater willingness to experiment with sexual variations*

◆ *Lessened inhibitions and increased ability to have fun during lovemaking*

◆ *Far greater technical proficiency as a lover.*

For couples there are close links between deepening sexual intimacy, relationship generally and friendship. Progress in any one of these areas will benefit the other two. Getting to the golden era can take months or years, but the journey offers many delights as well as a few heartaches. This section highlights some of the key parts of this journey, but it's just an overview. For the journey itself, you at least need to work through a couple of the books in Resources and ideally work with a good teacher or therapist. For example, some tantra teachers offer relationship training involving several residential groups over one to two years plus homework, and I've found this structure really helpful. A programme of sessions for you and your partner with a couples therapist can also be valuable.

While there's probably a lot of healing and learning you can do individually, the best sexual relationship needs change and outside support for you *and* your partner: some separately, but much of it together. Some women will be delighted to go this way with you, but not all. Some women have deep fears of intimacy, a need for control, maybe sexual wounds in earlier life that they can't bear to face. If so, you may face a tough decision on how patient to be and whether to miss out on this full depth in your relationship.

One of the great things about this life stage is that male and female preferences which seem incompatible for younger adults are changing. Research studies show that whereas younger men focus much more on sex than love, this reverses in midlife. While older women, from the forties onwards, have hormonal shifts which increase libido. Older women are typically more sexually assertive and more willing to experiment. So where's the highway to these golden years? Here are some of the landmarks:

◆ *Sexual self-confidence* is a fundamental need for both partners, and you need to help each other to find it, especially if the sex has gone stale. A loss of sexual self-esteem in the maturing years is understandable for both men and women. Problems like losing erections or vaginal dryness can hit us hard. Wrinkles, bulges and grey hair often upset us more than they do our partners. If your sexual self-confidence is low, the best single antidote is to focus on delighting your partner sexually. You should soon realise this is readily doable, and your confidence will increase with their pleasure.

◆ *Learn the art of sexual communication.* You and your partner need to learn how, when and where to talk with each other about sex, and how not to. You each need the skill to ask for and get what you want without the other feeling judged or nagged.

◆ *Use sacred space.* This is not just the usual suspects (candles, flowers, incense), although they're important. It means jointly using your intention to create a safe space where everyday worries are excluded, where you focus on love for each other and bring in the spiritual aspect of your connection. For example, Linda and I have a weekly appointment, a whole evening of intimate lovemaking, and we start by invoking what we call the angel of the relationship.

◆ *Fighting can unleash your sexuality.* If negative feelings like anger or jealousy are building up unexpressed between you and your partner, it can grind the sexual relationship to a halt. There are ways to express these feelings which free up the sexual energy trapped in them, without having an ordinary argument. For example, ranting at each other in gibberish, having a play fight without words, bashing cushions as you scream your heads off, can release the rage and leave you feeling pretty sexy.

◆ *You need technique!* This may sound distasteful, but it's crucial. Technique can make a huge difference in the level of ecstasy you both reach and it's also vital in turning some of the problems of ageing to advantage.

◆ *Experiment and play.* Especially in a long-term partnership, you need to find ways of renewing the passion and having fun. There are endless ways to do this, some may horrify you (or your partner), some may work brilliantly. For example: blindfolds, dressing up, acting out fantasies, watching sexy movies, going on a blind date as if you'd never met each other, simple playfulness...

◆ *Find the eyes of the heart.* At times, sex between middle-aged or older couples can feel vulnerable or ridiculous. You need to be careful and loving with each other.

◆ *Trust is the bedrock.* If there's a lack of trust in your partnership, you have to clear this: get outside help if necessary. Sexual trust is an especially delicate quality: it means trusting that when you are fully intimate together, your partner is not going to judge you, shame you or abuse you. Remember that your fears of such things probably come from the past, so don't project them onto the current situation.

◆ *Romance works.* Heartfelt romantic words and acts will always sweeten the relationship and the sexual connection. If you feel reluctant to go there, look at your own hang-ups and try to get past them. The Harville Hendrix book listed in Chapter 3 Resources is a great support for this.

FIRST SLOW FOOD, NOW SLOW SEX

The Slow Food Movement began in Italy, as a reaction against the poor quality of fast food. In Slow Food, fresh local ingredients and traditional recipes are used. The whole process of preparing, cooking and eating the food is unhurried, to be enjoyed at every stage. A lot of youthful sex is fast sex. It may be exciting, but wow, was that it? It's over already... If you look for the upside of the changes in male sexuality described above, it all points towards slow sex, which is what most women have been craving for years...

Remember the car comparison earlier in the book: at this age, you're a vintage classic, not a Grand Prix racer. Don't expect 0–60 in four minutes: enjoy the journey, have a picnic on the way. A lot of men like to give and receive a limited range of moves, with predictable results. Beyond fifty, responses are slower and less certain: it's a good time to let go of your performance anxiety, and enjoy experiments, uncertainty and receptiveness.

Slow sex is not an idea I just made up: you can find magazine features and even a book on it. However, this section is my personal take, drawing on many years of tantra. Central to my version is the Valley Orgasm: what's elegant about this is that losing your erection is a desirable part of the scenario. You alternate active and passive phases of lovemaking. At the end of the first period of active lovemaking, stop before the man ejaculates: this is where losing your erection is totally appropriate. Then rest together in this lovely state of sexual excitement, and use methods like visualisation and directed breathing to spread the intense sexual energy from the genitals through the body.

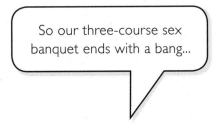

So our three-course sex banquet ends with a bang...

After a while, move into a second phase of active lovemaking: once again, continue until the man loses his erection or is close to ejaculation, or you just feel it's time to stop. Rest once more, spread the energy, and then if you want, go for a third phase of active lovemaking, which can include ejaculation. My experiences of this process have been truly amazing. You may worry that, once you've lost your erection, it may take a long time to get it back. My experience is that in this mix of a deeply loving space and high arousal, it will happen easily, but trust that it really won't matter either way.

There are some striking statistics about the average time that men of any age are in thrusting mode before ejaculation (three to five minutes) and the length of time a woman needs to become fully aroused (twenty minutes). Now factor in two partners of maturing years, and this could be heaven or this could be hell... Here's my slow sex scenario for a heavenly time:

◆ Set the scene: candles, incense, music, sacred space...

◆ The woman starts with slow, loving, sensual massage for the man, but avoiding the genital area.

◆ The man gives slow, loving, sensual massage to the woman, which can move on to sexual foreplay.

◆ Once the woman feels well aroused, she gives sexual stimulation to the man and you move together into the Valley Orgasm process, described above.

This kind of lovemaking is a great lesson in life generally for men: *You're not in control, you don't have to perform, the journey is what matters and the destination is unknown.* If you'd like to try the Valley Orgasm, buy the Margot Anand book listed in Resources, and go right through it, doing most of the exercises and rituals, which will prepare you for the Valley Orgasm.

Making love like this needs both of you to be fully present *and* fully surrendered. This can be difficult, especially if you have fears of intimacy, as most of us do. You may feel overwhelmed, scared or hit by old distress. If so, be gentle with each other, focus on what you need right now and be willing to switch from sexiness to supporter. Treat every lovemaking as an adventure, without expecting an outcome. This can be a great way to heal your fears of intimacy.

I'm not suggesting that you make love like this every time. One of my favourite tantra teachers, Sarita, says, 'Think of sex like food. You should know how to create and enjoy a banquet, but you don't want it every night. Enjoy variety, sometimes a quickie is just what you want.'

UNPACKING THE T WORD: TANTRA!

Tantra is a word I avoid when possible. It has been hijacked and distorted, and used as a projection for so many weird fantasies. Even when you dig into the truth of tantra, it takes so many forms that the one word hardly contains them. Here's a simple overview by Martin Jelfs, one of the leading UK tantra teachers:

> Because tantra is a mystical tradition it is very hard to define. In essence tantra is transformation and can be linked to alchemy: the transformation of the everyday into the divine. It is a spiritual science and the Hindu and Buddhist scriptures known as tantras give instructions on a wide range of topics including science, astronomy and rituals. The tantric texts include dialogues between the cosmic couple Shiva and Shakti: male and female tantric adepts.
>
> The central methods of tantra all include some way of transforming energy to aid spiritual evolution and a practice (as it usually is practiced within the Tibetan Buddhist tradition) involving detailed visualisation, sitting meditation, breathing and ritual. Or it can be done externally using a partner. This explains why some modern books on tantra are very much concerned with sexual practices and others don't even mention sex in the index! In either form the aim is the same: union with the divine. What can certainly be said is that tantra is affirming of the body, the senses and sexuality. In the tradition of sexual tantra, sometimes called the Left-hand Path, the body is experienced as the temple of the divine and the bridge between heaven and earth, spirit and matter.

I won't try to sum up tantra in this brief section, but here are a few typical teachings to help you decide if you want to explore it further:

◆ Treat your body and your partner's as a temple. This means taking care of your body through good diet, exercise, etc, and also getting through layers of shame and hang-ups about bulges, wrinkles, penis size, breast size and all that.

◆ Energy follows awareness and intention. This may sound

vague, but it has exciting implications for intensifying and directing sexual and spiritual energy. For example, you can use methods like breathing and visualisation to channel Kundalini energy from the sexual area right up the spine, which can give you an amazing full-body orgasm.

◆ Most tantra teaching advises men to learn how to retain semen, how to refrain from ejaculating. This enables you to channel, intensify and recirculate your sexual energy, whereas ejaculation is a simple one-way discharge.

◆ The masculine and feminine principles are often called Yin and Yang in tantra: it's important for each partner to honour both aspects in themselves and each other, and to bring both qualities fully into the relationship and lovemaking.

◆ Tantra processes often involve 'bodywork': physical movements which can help you release blocks and tensions (emotional and physical), raise the energy charge in the body, and create a sense of openness and flow which helps intimacy.

◆ One difference between most tantra and therapy processes is that tantra puts the focus on how you would like things to be, on strengthening the positive, whereas therapy encourages people to go more deeply into old, painful emotions. Linked to this, there is a lot of fun and playfulness in tantra groups and tantric sex.

◆ You can learn a lot of amazing techniques in tantra, and even some kinky sex positions, but the focus is usually on integrating the sexual connection with the heart and spirit.

Don't ever worry that you're too old for tantra: I've done a lot of tantra groups with a range of teachers and have always found them totally inclusive for all ages. It's common to find single men and couples in their fifties, sixties and seventies in these groups.

CROUCHING TIGRESS, HIDDEN DRAGON: LOVING A MENOPAUSAL WOMAN

The average age for menopause in the UK is fifty-one, so at some stage most maturing men will find themselves with a menopausal partner. During my fifties, I had several partners at different stages of the menopause. This confirmed what I've found in books: the way it affects women varies a lot, but most women are poorly prepared when it hits them. So if your partner is approaching the magic age, but is in denial, you can help by encouraging her to read one of the books in Resources.

Some of the issues affecting men beyond fifty are big for women too, and can make the menopause a midlife crisis, not just a physical change. For example, this is a time when kids leaving home or never having had children can lead to depression; when questions about life purpose and legacy can come to the fore. The menopause is often an emotional and spiritual crisis for a woman, and hopefully your experience with this book means you can support your partner through it.

> **How many menopausal women does it take to change a light bulb? None: the hot flushes light up the room.**

For sexual relations, the most difficult symptom is vaginal dryness, which is only suffered by a minority of women in menopause. However, it can cause serious distress for them and partners, a bit like erectile problems for men, with a similar risk of losing self-confidence. If you're used to your partner getting turned on and juicy quickly, this could be a blow to *your* self-confidence too, and a great chance to explore slow sex (see above). When this happens, you or your partner may blame it on emotional tension between you, or loss of libido: they can cause this problem sometimes, but at menopause there is a clear physiological reason: the drop in oestrogen levels.

A good response to these problems is to put more emphasis on love and touch, and less on penetrative sex.

Dryness problems can cause a woman to believe she has lost her sexuality forever: reassurance, tenderness and patience from you will help. You could also tell her that you know many women feel like this, but then discover the joys of mature sexuality. Explain that you know this from friends and books, not direct experience! Vaginal dryness can also be resolved short-term by lubricants, but be selective which ones you use. Herbal supplements and vitamins can help with this problem, such as aloe vera juice and vitamin C.

You may find it helpful to read one of the books on menopause in Resources, but here's an executive summary:

◆ The medical definition of menopause is a woman's last period. Many of the symptoms actually occur during *peri-menopause*, which can start sometime *before* the last period.

◆ The most common symptom is hot flushes, which are often linked with sleeplessness and irritability. Hot flushes are aggravated by chocolate and alcohol, but you may prefer that your partner learns this from a book...

◆ Good habits of diet and exercise before the menopause can greatly reduce the symptoms, and will also help during menopause and beyond.

◆ Other symptoms for a fair percentage of women include depression, anxiety, lack of energy and weight gain. There are good ways to deal with all of these, but motivation may be the first challenge.

RESOURCES

You may be reluctant to use outside advice, such as books and websites, but it really is worthwhile.

Physiology: Soft facts

For a short factual review of the basics, see www.health.msn.com, and search under 'male sexuality and ageing' for the piece by Harvey Simon.

The best sexual years of your life

Sex Over 50, by Joel Block. ISBN 978-0399534362. This book is excellent: clear, constructive and well-organised, covering many of the topics in this whole chapter. It covers both emotional issues and technique, enlivened by some juicy case studies.

Mars and Venus in the Bedroom, by John Gray. ISBN 978-0091887667. If you want a basic guide to the topic that's easy for both of you to read, try this.

Sex and relationship

Many of the resources for this chapter, and for Chapters 3 and 7, may also be relevant for these issues.

DIY Sex & Relationship Therapy, by Lori Boul. ISBN 978-1845284749. A delightfully clear, positive self-help book designed for couples to work through together. It has a cheerful, no-jargon approach and covers key topics, including basic communication and handling conflicts, with a good long section on sexual issues, including healing processes.

Healing Sex: A Mind-Body Approach to Healing Sexual Trauma, by Staci Haines. ISBN 978-1573442930. A well-rated, self-help workbook which aims to clear the impact of sexual abuse on current sex life. There's also a good section for partners.

Sexual Healing Journey: A Guide for Survivors of Sexual Abuse, by Wendy Maltz. ISBN 978-0062130730. A popular, well-written self-help book, good at relating current sexual problems to past issues. Parts of the process are to be done alone, but it also covers sexual healing with your partner, and has an extensive Resources section.

College of Sexual and Relationship Therapists: A UK professional organisation with about 750 members. The website has a lot of good briefing material and enables you to find a suitable therapist on their list. See: www.cosrt.org.uk.

Mind: A good gateway site, with briefings and organisation listings for sexual and other abuse problems. See: www.mind.org.uk.

Slow sex and tantra

Tantric Love, by Sarita and Geho. ISBN 978-1856751476. This offers the same approaches which Sarita teaches in her tantra workshops, with clearing emotional and physical blocks as a prelude to deeper intimacy. The book explains the principles of tantra concisely and clearly, and has a good sequence of self-guided exercises.

The Art of Sexual Ecstasy: Following the Path of Sacred Sexuality, by Margot Anand. ISBN 978-0007163830. A well-written and illustrated book by one of the leading teachers who has brought sexual tantra from East to West. Well designed as a self-guided process for a couple exploring sacred sexuality, although it helps to have the support of a tantra teacher and learning group on the journey. Be warned: the approach is quite full-on, quite New Age, and may not suit everyone.

Tantric Quest: An Encounter with Absolute Love, by Daniel Odier. ISBN 978-0892816200. Unlike the other two books listed here, this is not a self-help guide to tantra for Western couples. It's a vivid and moving story of a Frenchman's quest in the Himalayas for the true Eastern roots of tantra, and the spiritual and sexual awakening he found.

Celtic Tantra: Robert Osborn and Marta Emmit are a leading UK tantra teaching couple, and Celtic tantra is an approach which I have helped them to evolve at Hazel Hill Wood. I highly recommend their tantra groups as a safe way to start and then deepen your journey. See: www.celtictantra.com.

Tantra Essence: This is the website for Ma Ananda Sarita, a leading international tantra teacher. I have taken part in many of her groups and highly recommend her. Her website includes a lot of useful information and resources. See: www.tantra-essence.com.

Tantra: This is the website for Martin Jelfs, a UK tantra teacher quoted in the chapter. His website has useful material explaining what tantra is about. See: www.tantra.uk.com.

Menopause

Your Change, Your Choice, by Michael Dooley and Sarah Stacey. ISBN 978-0340828861. A clear and positive book which looks at all aspects of the menopause: physical, emotional and spiritual, recognising it as a major life change. Plenty of good advice about diet, herbal supplements, vitamins and how to tackle a range of symptoms, including sexual problems.

Women's Health Concern: If you search this site under menopause, you will find a range of useful articles about aspects of the menopause, including sexual relations. See: www.womens-health-concern.org.

You may not find much help for male partners on the internet, but try www.medicinenet.com, and search for the following article: 'The Men's Guide to Understanding Menopause' with Dick Roth. It's a helpful and entertaining account of how he supported his wife through her menopause.

Other resources

Taoist Secrets of Love: Cultivating Male Sexual Energy, by Mantak Chia and Michael Winn. ISBN 978-0943358192. This is nearly 300 pages of boggling technical detail by a leading expert on Taoist sexual teachings. It has whole sections on semen retention and Valley Orgasm, and numerous muscle and breathing exercises to increase your sexual agility, such as the scrotal compression exercise. You may want to take professional advice before embarking on some of these...

The Sexual Herbal, by Brigitte Mars. ISBN 978-1594772863. This is written for all ages and both genders, and offers a wide-ranging guide to this field, including homeopathy and vitamins as well as herbs, with a good troubleshooting section.

Livestrong: This website includes some useful information about herbs, vitamin supplements, diet and other ways to assist male sexuality. See: www.livestrong.com.

Chapter 11

Maturing organically:
Giving back as an elder

We shall not cease from exploration
And the end of all our exploring
Will be to arrive where we started
And know the place for the first time.
Through the unknown, remembered gate
When the last of earth left to discover
Is that which was the beginning.

T. S. ELIOT

So here we are, you the reader and me the author, at the last chapter, the home straight. Let's imagine we're sitting by a campfire at Hazel Hill Wood, on a clear October evening. The stars are sparkling overhead, the leaves are on the trees but turning gold. There's a coolness in the air: winter is not far away.

This is a good time to ponder your future and what you want from it. Do you reckon you have plenty of years of health and choice ahead of you? Or does it feel like time is short and you don't have much room for manoeuvre? Whether you reckon your future in months, years or decades, believe that you *can* shape the time ahead to be the way you want it. Hopefully the chapters before this have helped you to clear issues which were pulling you down, and to move forward in areas like work, health and relationships.

The focus of this chapter is on the bigger picture, legacy and giving back. We live in times of huge change and crisis: how does all this fit with your life? Could you help to address some of these challenges? The problems may seem so huge that you feel irrelevant, but we'll explore how to face them, and how you might make a difference – including scope for the elders to act together. This chapter also offers ways to apply sustainability to your own life and work, as well as the environment.

Somewhere between your fifties and eighties, the question of legacy will come up. How do you hope to be remembered when you're gone? Maybe you just want to be warmly regarded by those close to you – that's already a big thing. But you may want to make a difference, leave something behind you. In a huge world that's changing fast, this may seem a wild hope: for your own sanity, believe that every individual matters and every positive step is worthwhile, however small.

Many people feel so overwhelmed by the troubles of our times that they ignore them. Researchers have found that the commonest response to environmental crises is just switching off. I believe that a factor in many men's depression and addictions is that they can't face the awfulness and complexities of the society we live in and the planet we live on. As T. S. Eliot wrote, 'Humankind cannot bear very much reality.'

As you move into the retirement years, you may want to focus on hobbies, sports, telly, grandchildren... Fair enough, but do so as a conscious choice, not an avoidance or a refuge. Looking ahead, considering what you want, and what you want to leave behind, can help you make choices you won't regret later.

MEET THE WORLD LIKE A TREE: ROOTS THEN BRANCHES

As many people observe, mainstream media is focused on bad

news: crimes, scandals and disasters. And with instant access to gloom around the globe, they deluge us. No wonder people switch off and suffer from compassion fatigue. This section offers you a way to keep yourself rooted and face the world without being drowned in despair. Consider how plants grow: they build a root structure before they go above ground. In storms, wind or drought, their roots give them stability and nourishment. This is a useful model for human growth too, and here's how you could apply it for yourself:

Step 1: *Cultivate a strong, centred sense of self.* If you accept yourself, let go of old wounds, feel clear who you are and what your values are, you have a strong root to grow from. See Chapters 2 and 8 for help.

Step 2: *Grow your community connections.* These are like the network of fibres that anchor roots into the earth. In human terms, community becomes vital as we face ever-greater change and disruption. We need the mutual support and capacity for action that groups have compared to individuals. You may have several communities, such as friends, family, neighbours, colleagues and those who share your deeper values. Although it's easy now to have virtual groups online, try to keep many of your contacts local and face to face.

Step 3: *Manage your relationships to the bigger realities.* Just as seedlings are protected until strong enough to be planted out, protect yourself from being drowned and desensitised by mainstream media. This doesn't mean denial or escapism: you'll find good methods in this chapter and its resources which enable you to see the issues, but constructively and in managed doses. Steps 1 and 2 are a crucial prelude to this.

Facing the problems calmly

You may be surprised or even annoyed at the way this chapter is going. Wasn't it meant to be about giving back, doing good and positive stuff? We'll get to that, but the skills to face the issues are a vital step.

Good insights come from Joanna Macy, who calls herself an eco-philosopher and spiritual activist. She is intense but clear and relevant. For example:

> *The cause of our apathy, however, is not indifference. It stems from a fear of the despair that lurks beneath the tenor of life-as-usual... Because of social taboos against despair and because of fear of pain, it is rarely acknowledged or expressed directly... The energy expended in pushing down despair is diverted from more creative uses, depleting the resilience and imagination needed for fresh visions and strategies. Fear of despair erects an invisible screen, filtering out anxiety-provoking data. In a world where organisms require feedback in order to adapt and survive, this is suicidal.*

For details of her books and website, see Resources.

Her approach combines the science of ecology with nature-based spiritual teachings from Buddhism and the Native Americans. Joanna Macy has a clear, simple method to help us face the big issues and find our ability to act on them. In summary, it is:

1. Opening to gratitude
2. Owning our pain for the world
3. Seeing with new eyes
4. Going forth.

She explains that this is a four-step cycle which we need to spiral round repeatedly, maybe daily, not as some one-off transformation. Let's explore each step in more detail:

1. *Opening to gratitude.* Whatever your challenges and worries may be, try shifting your focus to thankfulness: for the gift of life itself and all the resources that keep you alive. Include the many

gifts of nature, such as food and beauty, and the good things you receive from other people: friends, family and the huge array of workers we all depend on. Starting with gratitude helps us to be present in the here and now, to relax and open up beyond our worries. As Joanna Macy says:

Thankfulness loosens the grip of the industrial growth society by contradicting its predominant message: that we are insufficient and inadequate. The forces of late capitalism continually tell us that we need more – more stuff, more money, more approval, more comfort, more entertainment.

2. *Owning our pain for the world.* This stage can be tough: it helps to find a group or mentor to start it with. Macy's books contain excellent rituals and other methods to help you do this, both alone and with others. Most of us stuff down and deny the pain we feel at the ways that the earth and its creatures are being abused and destroyed. It takes courage to face your pain, it can be distressing, but this step should enable you to move into the next two.

3. *Seeing with new eyes.* By letting yourself feel your pain for the world, you open up to a new sense of connection with that world and with other people. Macy calls this *a shift in identification... from the isolated 'I' to a vaster sense of what we are.* This is a crucial prelude to the fourth step: as small, solitary egos, we are right to feel powerless. When we feel ourselves as part of the living network of life and part of a community, something different becomes possible.

4. *Going forth.* This is the stage of taking action: maybe as an individual, maybe with others. Macy describes this as *the discovery of what can happen through us... one simply finds oneself empowered to act on behalf of other beings – or on behalf of the larger whole.*

Facing the world is arduous: it's worth spending time on these preparatory, rooting steps, so you don't get overwhelmed when you start to look around and take action. The next sections consider two of the biggest problem areas of our times: social and environmental issues.

BIG ISSUES 1: SOCIAL

There are always lots of social issues to address: big and small, global and local. My tip is to follow your passion: find a way to help resolve the problems that touch you deeply. And don't start from despair; there's good news and progress on some fronts, but we rarely hear about it. When you're reading or watching the news, notice which topics affect you most and consider getting involved. This may mean gifting your time or money, but don't rule out finding paid work on a project you care about. Parts of Chapter 4 can help with this.

This section won't cover all the issues or all the ways you can contribute. It offers highlights on both points and there's more in Resources. Don't approach this area with a mood of self-sacrifice: believe there are ways to meet your needs *and* help others. It's more healthy and sustainable if there's a two-way exchange, so be clear what you'd like to receive, as well as what you can give: for example working with others or learning new skills.

Local webs are stronger than virtual ones

Compare your life now to five or ten years ago: how much of your social contact, shopping and information-gathering has shifted from local, face to face or voice to voice, to virtual and screen-based through your computer and smartphone? It's worth pulling the balance back towards local: it strengthens the community around you and you'll benefit from this if the crises which some are forecasting actually happen, for example:

◆ Breakdown of internet and mobile phone networks, for example because satellites are knocked out by changes in Earth magnetism.

◆ Shortages of oil and huge price rises force us to rely on local food and other supplies.

◆ More widespread riots force local communities to support each other and face the underlying issues.

A worthwhile and effective way to strengthen a local community is for people in the neighbourhood to work together to tackle a local problem. There's already a lot of this happening: some in ongoing groups and some responding to a crisis, like floods or the clean-up groups after the riots of 2011.

Finding out what groups or projects are active in your locality may be tricky. Some will be so informal or short-term that they won't show up on a web search. Some may be linked to churches or other faith groups, but that doesn't necessarily mean that you have to share these beliefs. Here are a few ways to see where you could get involved:

◆ Read the local paper for news on relevant organisations.

◆ Look at parish newsletters, local notice boards, and What's On listings for relevant meetings or events.

◆ Contact national organisations that could be relevant (Age UK, for example) and find out if they have a local branch.

◆ Check the website for the Facing the 2020s project I've started on raising community resilience: www.living-organically.com/2020s.html.

Mentoring younger men

If there was a corner shop offering issues for older men to help with, this should be in the front window: our presence is uniquely important. Crime, drugs and education are among many areas where young men have worse problems than young women: for example, 80% of kids excluded from schools are boys. Two-thirds of all male criminal offenders are under thirty. Men are twice as likely as women to have used any drug, and Class A drug use is highest among twenty to twenty-nine-year old men.

It's clear that the lack of fathering and older male role models have been a major factor in these problems, and mentoring for young men can help. Put simply, it involves an ongoing supportive relationship with an older man who has suitable skills and experience. It's not therapy, and it's not really a fathering role. In traditional tribal societies, initiation and guidance of young men didn't come from their fathers, but from the elders of the tribe.

To give you an idea of what mentoring can mean to a young man, here is a quote from one of them:

> *My name is Bilal... I started getting into trouble with the police when I was thirteen years old. For the next three years I was in trouble for fighting, drinking alcohol, causing criminal damage, arson and joyriding stolen cars... With A Band of Brothers, I did the initial weekend training and got a mentor called Peter who's a painter and decorator that lives in the same neighbourhood as me. I met with Pete every week and he helped me to believe that I could achieve my dream of becoming a mechanic one day... Pete also supported me to go to the weekly groups with A Band of Brothers where I learned better ways of dealing with conflict and expressing my emotions... I am now nine months into my three-year apprenticeship and on track to becoming a fully fledged technician. (Source: www.abandofbrothers.org.uk)*

Back in the 1990s, I was part of a team at The Magdalen Project, the educational charity I founded, who tried to do mentoring for young men in trouble. We quickly found that well-intentioned but untrained amateurs get into difficulties very fast. A good mentoring programme needs to engage the hearts and souls of those involved, but also has to be well organised and quality-controlled to earn the confidence of the clients and the statutory bodies involved. A Band of Brothers and Journeyman UK, listed in Resources, are two organisations whose programmes supporting young men are well designed and maintained.

Many mentoring programmes are for young men in trouble, but there's also a need for mentoring young men who are a bit lost and unsupported. The Prince's Trust and Community Service Volunteers offer ways to help in this area. If you're in a local men's group, you might explore what you could do together. One men's group in Devon looked for young men locally needing support and found examples like these:

◆ A twenty-two-year old needing support and advice after his father died suddenly.

◆ An eighteen-year old whose relationship with his father had broken down after several years of arguing. Support for both of them helped to restore the relationship.

BIG ISSUES 2: ENVIRONMENTAL

The ongoing global crisis of the environment can be easy to ignore: many people turn away because they can't cope with facing it. Politicians mostly say the right things but don't do much: effective action would require short-term pain for long-term gain, coordinated between many countries internationally, which is hardly a vote-winner. What I mean by the environmental crisis includes:

◆ The likely increase in average global temperatures by over 2°C by 2050, implying major losses of productive farmland, big rises in sea level and much more.

◆ Forecasts within the oil industry that global oil production in 2030 will be 90% below the 2010 level. Even if the drop is 70% or 80%, this implies major price rises, supply cuts, economic setbacks and probably riots.

◆ Water shortages already seriously affect over 20% of world population and this is likely to pass 40% by 2040.

◆ Pollution and other human activities are continuing to cause rapid loss of habitats across the world.

If you're already switching off and despairing, go back to the processes earlier in this chapter. *We can all do something!* In my experience, the best approach is to focus on a couple of issues, organisations or locations. Ensure that some of this involves a real place or group of people near you. For example, there's probably a Wildlife Trust or similar body running nature reserves near you that needs conservation help. If your passion is to campaign about the global issues, some organisations like Friends of the Earth have local groups across the country. In many local communities Transition Towns are creating practical green initiatives. There are so many environmental issues and organisations that it's impossible to cover the field. I've highlighted a couple here.

Peak oil and the Hubbert Curve

You may have heard the term 'peak oil', which highlights the probability that global oil production is near its peak, and that global demand will increasingly outstrip the diminishing supply. The Hubbert Curve is used within the oil industry to forecast net production: do a web search and the results will probably shock you. They suggest that global oil production peaked around 2011 and that by the year 2035 production will have dropped to 10% of the peak level. Take a few minutes to sit with this: the implications are so huge that they're hard to imagine. That's true even if the drop is only to 20% or it takes another few years.

Most experts say it's impossible for alternative energy sources, such as wind and sun, to make up this shortfall. They may fill some of the gap, but we must be heading for large reductions in global energy use and huge rises in the cost of oil and oil-derived products such as plastics, fertilisers and many more. Demand for oil is pretty inelastic, ie there are no quick, easy substitutes and the activities which consume it can't readily be cut back. This means that as output declines, prices will be bid up very fast. Predictions like this aren't new, but now they are more authoritative, more imminent, and we've already had a foretaste: remember 2008 when oil hit $145 a barrel? Within ten or twenty years, oil could be above $500 a barrel, and poorer countries may struggle to get supplies.

I'm basically an optimist, but we have to face the fact that there are radical threats to everyone's quality of life over the next couple of decades, of which peak oil is only one. There's a real possibility that peak oil alone could lead to economic depression and shortages of fuel and food sparking riots and anarchy, even in the UK. We can't prevent the pressures, but we can increase our resilience by reducing our dependence on fossil fuels, increasing self-sufficiency, and giving our local communities the skills and togetherness to face such shocks.

The Transition Network

I want to highlight Transition because it's trying to create the kind of local responses which I'm advocating. Its initiator is Rob Hopkins, and it's worth reading his books. The Transition Movement looks for constructive responses and builds local networks which are sociable as well as practical. This may sound obvious, but some environmental organisations have a gloom-laden outlook, focus entirely on the task and leave you ashamed if you ever drive a car. The downside of Transition Town is that it's so hands-off: local groups are free to do their own thing, and vary widely in how active and relevant to their locality they are. Some local groups are terrific and some are disappointing, but it's worth a try.

Farm Africa: Systemic answers at the grass roots

I'm highlighting this smallish UK-based charity because I have worked with them, and to show that there's more good news out there than you may think. In 2011, I visited Ethiopia with my younger daughter, who was assessing UK Government aid programmes there. Instead of going as a tourist, I wanted my trip to help others and enable me to meet local people in a different way.

Farm Africa works in several countries, including Ethiopia, helping small farmers and foresters to adapt to changing environmental and economic conditions. For example, they train smallholders to cope with drought through different seeds and tilling methods. With my interest in woodlands from Hazel Hill, I set up a field visit to their large sustainable forestry programme in the Bale region of south-east Ethiopia. This is a large, rare area of tropical alpine forest, which was being rapidly deforested until Farm Africa's programme.

What impresses me about all Farm Africa's work is that they seek systemic answers and transfer good ideas and techniques from one continent or country to another. In the Bale Forest I found all the bright initiatives I could have imagined, and many more, actually working. For example, they understood how to set up legal structures which fitted both Government policies and traditional villages. These enable villages to register as producer cooperatives which can obtain a lease to manage their local forest. The result is that villages can earn more from products like wild honey, forest coffee and bamboo furniture than by felling the forest and keeping livestock.

The pilot programmes were so successful that this has been rolled out to cover 740,000 acres, with even larger rollouts under way. I'm using Farm Africa as an example of thousands of organisations we're not aware of, doing invaluable work on environmental and other issues around the world. These organisations all need to raise more funds and more awareness of the issues they are tackling. Many of them, including Farm Africa, have local groups and a range of ways that you can help them within your own neighbourhood.

HOW TO MATURE ORGANICALLY: LIVING SUSTAINABLY

Organic farming produces higher-quality food by sustainable methods: it doesn't deplete natural resources, it renews them.

By contrast, conventional farming relies on artificial fertilisers and pesticides, many derived from fossil fuels, which deplete the earth's fertility, and leave soil and groundwater polluted. Human sustainability is just as important as environmental, and the principles and methods of organic growth can be translated from farms to people. This is the subject of my first book, *The Natural Advantage: Renewing Yourself*, which is a practical guide to doing this in your life and work.

As we grow older, our bodies may be polluted by years of stress, lack of exercise and so on. Our metabolisms slow down, so our ability to clear such problems is less, and living sustainably should be a priority in our maturing years. It took me a whole book to show how people can apply organic growth in their life and work, but here's a quick overview:

The seven principles of organic growth:

1. Ground condition

To organic farmers, soil quality is the source of sustainable output. They aim to improve the reserves and resilience of their soil while increasing its production. By contrast, conventional farming progressively depletes and pollutes the soil, so that output depends on ever-increasing external stimulants (fertilisers) and suppressants (pesticides). This offers ways to understand, improve and sustain our own ground condition, our reserves and resilience.

2. Natural energy

The main energy sources for organic farms are sunlight, water, earth, air and organic waste: natural, abundant, low-cost and non-polluting. Pushing yourself along with stress, fear and addictive stimulants (such as alcohol) is like using fossil fuels: it builds up residues that lower resilience and creativity. Recall times when you felt deeply appreciated or inspired – how energised you felt, how everything flowed more easily for you. There are simple ways to stimulate and harness these natural energies which don't have polluting side effects.

3. Composting waste

The beauty of natural cycles is that there's no waste: every output becomes the input to the next stage of the cycle. The waste in your life includes unresolved conflicts and negative feelings, such as anxiety and anger. Waste is usually messy: it takes new skills to collect and recycle it, but this can be done. Negativity can become a source of fresh understanding and constructive energy. Composting is a classic example of natural synergy: you get more out than you put in, and it provides a model of how to recycle wasted energy for people too.

4. Organic synergy: Growing through uncertainty

Organic farmers achieve results with less control and amid more uncertainty than anyone else I know. Synergy means getting one and one to make three or more, and organic farmers show us how to achieve this through creative tension: using uncertainty, finding the gift in the problem. By combining active intent and push with receptiveness and adaptability, we can harness change to create results. This is the co-creative approach: it's central to achieving goals amid change and uncertainty. Elements of co-creativity include tolerance for ambiguity, and developing both intuition and logic.

5. Using natural growth cycles

The organic approach doesn't 'let nature take its course', but works *with* it. Organic farmers use natural cycles, such as crop rotation and the four seasons. Applying this to your life and work, renew your energy by alternating between a stressful situation and an easy one, or between a structured and a fluid approach. Or treat your life as a repeating cycle of seeding-growing-harvesting-rest.

6. Resilience from diversity

Even small organic farms have a diverse range of products or enterprises. This creates resilience: if one crop fails or demand drops, the farm can survive the blow. The various crops support each other and create synergy. Diversity is key to reducing weed and pest problems. So are wild margins: uncultivated land supporting the birds and insects that keep pests in check. Diversity is vital for people too in our work, leisure and social life. Vary the approaches you take (eg active/passive, intuitive/analytical), and keep the wild margins in yourself and your network of contacts which can offer new solutions for the unexpected.

7. Real quality

When you eat a piece of fruit, how do you judge its quality? Real quality is about taste, nutrition and a feeling of satisfaction. Organic produce may look irregular, but it delivers real quality. Conventional farming is geared to deliver nominal quality: size, appearance, consistency and quantity.

An important feature of real quality is a flexible, two-way relationship between producer and customer. The rapport and trust in such relationships are part of the satisfaction the product delivers, and both parties are able to handle more change and uncertainty. Most large organisations focus on nominal quality, and the same trend is seen in call centres, chat rooms, gaming and the rise of the virtual world. Real quality means personal, local and ethical contacts in both personal and work life.

There are so many pressures in our society which push us round and round the cycle of feeling dissatisfied, consuming more stuff, and so increasing the problems of pollution and depletion: for ourselves and the planet. If you can start to live by the seven principles of organic growth described above, you'll not only be making your own life more sustainable, but helping others to see what's possible.

ENJOYING YOUR ELDERHOOD

There is, it seems to us,
At best, only a limited value
In the knowledge derived from experience.
The knowledge imposes a pattern, and falsifies,

For the pattern is new in every moment
And every moment is a new and shocking
Valuation of all we have been.

Do not let me hear
Of the wisdom of old men, but rather of their folly,
Their fear of fear and frenzy, their fear of possession,
Of belonging to another, or to others, or to God.
The only wisdom we can hope to acquire
Is the wisdom of humility: humility is endless.

T. S. ELIOT

So much of this chapter is about elders giving back and being of service that you may think that's what I believe elderhood is all about. Actually, I've concluded that each of us has to figure out our own form of elderhood and what being an elder means for us. This is different from the traditions of initiating adolescents *into* adulthood, where they are told their duties, roles and values. Initiation into elderhood is a more organic, gradual, self-guided process. You may learn from other elders as role models, they may give support, but the vision comes from you and any guiding spirits or divinity you work with. Here are some of the best ways to explore what elderhood means for you, and to move into it:

◆ Alone and in nature, for example the Wisdom Quest process described in Chapter 7.

◆ Sharing your exploration with other maturing men in a regular group or one-off events.

◆ Using dreams, meditation and other practices which help you open to the spiritual and unconscious aspect of yourself.

When does elderhood begin and finish? Every man's journey is unique. The age fifty is often a turning point. However, I've seen men with the wisdom of elderhood in their late twenties and men in their seventies who've not yet reached it. I believe that elderhood is a stage we find for ourselves, hopefully in our fifties or sixties and this stage of elderhood lasts until we die. There are others who see elderhood as followed by seniority, a stage of passing out of life and into death and whatever lies beyond.

To help your exploration, here are some brief pointers to aspects of elderhood:

Simple presence. If you're at ease with yourself, calm amid setbacks and focused on the positive, your presence alone will be a teaching and a role model for those around you of all ages.

Embodying and upholding values. This is a major role of tribal elders and much needed in our society. This means living the principles you believe in, such as honesty, integrity and forgiveness, and speaking out for these values when you see them ignored.

Elders as a group. In these later years, the balance between individual and collective life swings more towards the group: this means shared wisdom, mutual support and perhaps shared action too.

Friendship. Slowing down should be a goal and a benefit of elderhood. This creates time for you to be a friend to other elders, to your children and grandchildren, and wherever it's needed. Sharing your love, your wisdom and your values with others through friendship is part of your legacy.

Giving back, serving the greater good. This is covered at length earlier in the chapter, but I want to remind you to consider it!

Facing ageing and death. I was closest to my father, and learned most from him, in his last years and his death. I know many older men who have found the same. If you can find happiness even in your decline and face death positively, you create a blessing for yourself and younger generations.

Surrendering to the unconscious. If you have stayed aware, you must feel by now that the complexity inside and around you is so huge that you can't think your way to understanding. Surrendering to the unconscious is not giving up, it's opening to receive the wisdom within us and around us, which can't all be channelled through the rational mind.

Opening to the beyond. The years of elderhood are a chance to open to the world of spirit, to whatever lies beyond death. This is a fitting part of our later life and probably serves the tribe as well.

There are so many pressures pulling people and governments around the world towards the immediate, visible problems, which are often social and economic. Raising attention, speaking out, walking the talk, calling for action on the huge but less immediate crises of environmental *and* human sustainability, is a role that the elders need to take up. The elders are a big voice, a power for change, and without us stepping in, we're all on the road to hell.

RESOURCES

Both the topic of elderhood and the big issues of our times are moving rapidly, so it's worth searching for the latest books and websites, as well as those recommended below.

Four Quartets, by T. S. Eliot. ISBN 978-0571068944. All of the T. S. Eliot quotes in this chapter and the whole book come from this long poem, which contains a lot of wisdom about life, and elderhood in particular.

World as Lover, World as Self: A Guide to Living Fully in Turbulent Times, by Joanna Macy. ISBN 978-1888375718. A fairly accessible overview of Joanna Macy's key ideas and processes, and the source for my summary of her approach in this chapter.

Coming Back to Life: Practices to Reconnect Our Lives, Our World, by Joanna Macy. ISBN 978-0865713918. This provides an overview of some of Macy's key ideas, such as Living Systems Theory and Deep Ecology, and details of group processes which embody deep ecology: deepening our sense of what the natural world is calling for from the humans.

Find Your Power: A Toolkit for Resilience and Positive Change, by Chris Johnstone. ISBN 978-1856230506. Chris is a UK teacher and psychologist who has worked a lot with Joanna Macy. This is a highly rated self-help book which can help you to find the strength and clarity for inner and outer change.

Joanna Macy: Contains masses of information about Joanna Macy's key ideas and her writings about them, including material for study groups. See: www.joannamacy.net.

Chris Johnstone: Chris runs a range of events in the UK, based on his own material and Joanna Macy's teachings. This website includes event listings and excerpts from his writings. See: www. chrisjohnstone.info.

Big issues 1: Social

There are loads of books about the problems and how they could be solved. In some ways it's best just to make a start, so I am listing books and publications with some reservations.

Volunteering: The Essential Guide, by Leonie Martin ISBN 978-1861441331. This is a readable, down-to-earth UK guide on different kinds of volunteering roles and organisations, and how to get started.

Positive News: If you'd like a dose of encouraging info about progress, and constructive projects around the UK and beyond, subscribe to the quarterly newspaper, *Positive News,* and log onto www.positivenews.org.uk.

Resurgence & Ecologist: *Resurgence* magazine, published every two months, offers excellent constructive insights on social and environmental issues from leading sources, and they publish some excellent material on their website. See: www.resurgence. org.

Volunteering England: Operates a network of volunteer centres which are a good place to start. Their website lists ideas for volunteering in your local area, and a number of national charities who offer local volunteering opportunities. See: www.volunteering.org.uk.

Do–it: This is a well-organised website that has an excellent search facility to help you find opportunities in a wide range of volunteering sectors, either locally or elsewhere. See: www.do–it.org.uk.

Mentoring for young men is a small but growing sector in the UK, with much of it happening locally and informally. Here are some websites which may be useful:

A Band of Brothers: This is a smallish, newish UK charity. I rate their approach highly. See: www.abandofbrothers.org.uk.

Journeyman UK: This is the UK affiliate of an American organisation training older men to mentor younger men. It looks well organised and worthy of support. See: www.journeymanuk.org.

Prince's Trust: The Prince's Trust offers well-structured opportunities to mentor young people all around the UK: typically you would be supporting a young adult for a few hours per month over several months, after they have completed a structured training programme with the Prince's Trust. If you don't feel you have the skills and robustness to deal with young men in trouble, this could be a good place to try mentoring. See: www.princes-trust.org.uk.

Community Service Volunteers: This is a large charity offering a range of volunteering possibilities, including mentoring for young people. See: www.csv.org.uk.

Social Evils: Don't be put off by the word 'evils', it's more archaic than moralistic. This is an update of a public consultation originally carried out by a Quaker charity in 1904. It has a useful list of six major issues seen as priorities in a consultation of 3,500 people. See: www.socialevils.org.uk.

Big issues 2: Environmental

This is another field where looking for books or websites could leave you thoroughly confused. Many of the obvious websites to try, such as Friends of the Earth, focus on current campaigns and blogs, and don't give a good overview.

The State of the World Report, by Worldwatch Institute. This report is published annually by a highly reputable non-profit foundation in the US. It gives a good overview of environmental issues and analysis of good strategies to address them. See: www.worldwatch.org/bookstore/state-of-the-world

The Transition Companion: Making Your Community More Resilient in Uncertain Times, by Rob Hopkins. ISBN 978-1603583923. Rob is a brilliant and likeable guy who started the Transition Network and has been a key figure in its rapid growth. This is a 2011 update of his Transition Handbook: a superb assembly of methods, inspiration and case studies for community-led responses to peak oil and climate change.

Buzzle: This website gathers good material from the internet on a large variety of topics. If you search under 'Environment', their list of current environmental issues and top problems is good and clear. See: www.buzzle.com.

Friends of the Earth: One of the leading UK organisations campaigning for solutions to environmental problems. They have over 200 local groups, so this is a good way to make face-to-face contact with people concerned about sustainability. They also have a range of volunteering opportunities. See: www.foe.co.uk.

Transition Network: This website contains huge amounts of information about the whole transition network: aims, methods, and a directory of the large number of transition towns and other initiatives in the UK and beyond. See: www.transition-network.org.

Appendix 1

Work and money:
Self-guided exercises

1. Personal energy audit

This audit is designed to give you an overview of your main energy inflows and outflows, so you can set yourself priorities for managing your energy better and identify issues for investigation.

The audit is not exhaustive and not a substitute for professional help where needed, for example a medical health check, advice on diet and exercise tailored to your needs, or counselling on major emotional issues.

Use the checklist to assess the main energy inflows and outflows in your working life. The processes in which you *use* energy should be considered as outflows. The items listed are not meant to be comprehensive; space is provided to add other items significant to you. For each one, rate its importance on a scale of 0 (unimportant) to 10 (highly important). Put an asterisk in the Review Priority column for items you feel need urgent consideration. Remember that some items may be both a source and a use of energy.

Initially, do these ratings for your current way of working; you may wish to do the exercise again, to see how much impact a different approach would have. Remember that outflows include those that are desirable and productive, and those that dissipate or misuse energy.

	Energy inflow	Energy outflow	Review priority
PHYSICAL			
The activities of your work itself			
Other activity related to your work, eg commuting, preparing for work, winding down afterwards			
Diet: 'healthy', sustaining food/drink 'unhealthy' food/drink			
Breathing (deeper, relaxed is energizing)			
Exercise			
Relaxation			
Other:			
EMOTIONAL			
Self-appreciation or putdown: supporting or blaming yourself, eg when results are not 'successful'			
Appreciation or negativity from colleagues at work			
Feelings expressed towards you by people you work with (including colleagues or customers)			
The general attitude to feelings where you work: can feelings be voiced or are they suppressed?			
The emotional rewards or pressures of the whole organisation			
How do you respond to unexpected changes at work? Are they typically a stimulus or a stress for you?			
Support/antagonism from family and friends			
The emotional rewards or demands of your leisure time/hobbies			
Other:			

	Energy inflow	Energy outflow	Review priority
MENTAL			
Does the content of your work and the way you choose to do it give you mental stimulus or exhaustion?			
Does the organisation you work in give you mental stimulus or exhaustion?			
Is your habitual way of thinking positive and creative, or do you tend to worry and fret, and focus on the negatives?			
Do you use both logical and intuitive skills in your work and integrate them?			
Do uncertainty and conflicting data stimulate or dissipate your mental energy?			
Do you have activities outside work (eg family, friends, hobbies) that give you mental stimulus or exhaustion?			
Other:			
INSPIRATIONAL			
Do you have a sense of purpose and inspiration in your work?			
Does the organisation you work for/lead have a true sense of purpose and service that helps to inspire your work?			
Do you have a mentor, boss or colleague who is a role model for you in bringing spiritual energy to work?			

	Energy inflow	Energy outflow	Review priority
When your work gets demanding or exhausting, can you re-energize yourself by remembering the point of it all?			
Do you have a sense of purpose and inspiration in your life generally?			
In your free time, do you choose any activities that inspire you (eg through nature, music, meditation), or do you choose distractions or compensations for stress and fatigue?			
Other:			

2. Fantasy ticket

Let yourself imagine that there are no practical limits for you regarding money, age, health, qualifications or location. In this fantasy you're totally free to do the work you'd like to. No restrictions – wow! Pause and take this in. Now, ask yourself what is your ideal fantasy job, what the real you would truly like to do. Just shut your eyes and let something come to you...

Now describe your fantasy job in as much detail as you can. What things are you doing in a typical day? Who do you work with? Where? Describe the atmosphere and physical details of the place. What are you wearing? List the things you find most satisfying about this fantasy job. Describe the people you meet in it and the experiences it gives you. Who do you work for (if anyone) and how do you relate to them? You may want to draw a picture or write down details of your fantasy.

Now take time to review it and see what it tells you. You can do this alone or with a partner. Here are some questions to explore:

◆ What are your first feelings and responses to what came out for you?

◆ Describe the underlying needs, wants and desires which your fantasy job has shown you.

◆ How possible and achievable does your fantasy feel to you?

◆ How much of it could become possible in the future for you?

◆ Can you 'translate' your fantasy into a different form which would be possible, even if the original form doesn't seem to be?

◆ How would you feel, how would you be different, if you were actually doing a form of your fantasy job?

◆ What are the obstacles to this happening and how could you overcome them?

◆ How would you like to follow this up? What steps could you take to pursue this further?

3. Work/Life vision statement

Part I: Gathering insights

This exercise can help you get in touch with your vision for your life and work. Please complete all three questions below before moving on to Part II. Get relaxed, tune into your intuition, then just write down the answers that come to you! Don't worry if they look odd, impossible or contradictory. Underline any that strike you as especially important.

i) List qualities, strengths and abilities you value in yourself.

ii) List things you do which express yourself, activities or states in which you feel fulfilled, where you're really being yourself.

iii) Picture your ideal world. What would you like to have in it?

Part II: Putting your statement together

Begin by relaxing and tuning into your intuition. Take a few deep breaths. Feel in touch with your inner self, the part that knows what you want.

Now take the first section, and pick one quality that is your special quality, the essential you, the gift you value most in yourself. If it's hard to choose, try shutting your eyes and sitting quietly for a minute – see what your intuition tells you.

Next, take your second list, things you like doing, and choose the three that are most expressive or satisfying for you.

Now, take the third list, and choose the three bits you'd most like to have as part of your world. Don't spend time analysing, just go with the ideas that come first.

Now we're ready to put a statement together. Write:

'I express and apply my _____ (the one quality)

by _____
(the three things you like doing)

to bring forth _____

_____ (the three things you'd like in your world).

Try repeating your statement aloud to yourself. How does it make you feel? Does anything surprise you? You might write down your first reactions to this purpose statement, then spend time considering it.

4. The eight–six–three reality filter

Your starting point for this process should be the results of Fantasy Ticket and the Work–Life Vision Statement. Connect with the positive feelings about your vision: the inspiration and excitement. Ask the left and right sides of your brain to work together to give you clear, practical answers to the questions below.

i) Thinking about your fantasy work and your vision statement, list eight types of work which you could realistically do, which would give you some of the fulfilment and use the skills in your fantasy and vision.

ii) Looking at your list of eight work activities, choose the three which seem most possible and attractive to you. For each of these, write down two situations, projects or organisations where you might do this work activity.

iii) Looking at the list of six, pick the three which seem the most realistic and interesting to investigate. For each one, write down the practical steps you can take to do some work in this situation, and set yourself a target time.

5. Backcasting

This process is used in creating scenarios for sustainable development programmes. I have adapted it here to exploring a new area of work.

Check the timeframe you set for your work changes in the Re-visioning section A2 of Chapter 4. Connect with your fantasy job, vision statement and whatever specific ideas you have had about first steps.

Now take a few relaxing breaths and ask your intuition for a picture of yourself at work, at the end of your chosen timeframe. Explore this picture as fully as possible: what are you doing, who are you working with, where are you, how are you feeling? Now ask your intuition to bring you slowly back in time from this future picture towards the present. What key decisions and actions did you take between now and then? What got you there? Ask your intuition if there is any other information you need to make this picture a reality.

6. Outlook on work

Don't read ahead! This is a good exercise to uncover some underlying beliefs which you may be carrying about your work. Before you start, make sure you have at least fifteen minutes of quiet time, and a notepad and pen. If possible get a partner to read out these instructions for you, otherwise just continue on your own.

Picture yourself at work on a typical working day. Notice the physical details around you and try to feel the way you usually feel at work. Now go on to the first statement below. Say it out loud, and then see whatever comes next as you complete the statement. Write it down, repeat the start of the statement, complete it again. Keep going for at least twenty repetitions, and make sure you keep going through the point when you feel this is irritating or boring. Do the same for the second statement.

Statement 1: At work I should …

Statement 2: Work is …

Now review the way you completed both statements. Can you see some ongoing beliefs that colour your experience of work, and your beliefs about what's possible in future? Can you relate these to earlier experiences or other parts of your life? Consider ways you can change these beliefs so they don't limit your future choices.

7. Getting clearer about money

*This section offers you three processes to help you clarify your underlying beliefs and your relationship to money. **Don't read ahead!** Get some blank paper and a few pens, and do these processes when you have half an hour of uninterrupted time.*

a) *What's the picture?* Sit and relax, take some long, deep breaths and close your eyes after you have read this. Imagine that your money is an animal, a person or an object. Picture it as vividly as you can and feel the relationship between the two of you. Is your money bigger than you or smaller? Who is in charge here? How do you feel towards your money? How does your money feel about you? When you have a clear picture, draw the image and write down the insights.

b) *Ask the question*. This is a sentence completion exercise. Keep saying the following phrase and then write down whatever comes up to complete the sentence. Repeat this at least twenty times and push yourself through the stage when you think it is pointless.

Money is ...

c) *Exploring limitations*. If you feel a lack of money in your life, this process can help you understand why. It's another sentence completion process, so follow the instructions for b) above.

I can't get enough money because ...

Appendix 2

Addiction: Screening questions

These questions concern the past twelve months. Each question is answered 'yes' or 'no'. The questions can be used for any substance or behaviour. In this example we'll use cannabis.

- Did you find you needed more cannabis to get the desired effect or that the same amount has had less of an effect?

- Did you feel sick, unwell or just uncomfortable when the effects of cannabis wore off or did you take more of it or a similar drug to relieve or avoid feeling unwell (or just to feel generally better again)?

- Did you use cannabis in larger amounts or for a longer period of time than you intended?

- Would you say that you've had a persistent or strong desire to take cannabis?

- Did you spend a large amount of time obtaining/using or recovering from the effects of cannabis?

- Did you reduce or give up work, recreational or social activities as a result of your cannabis use?

- Did you continue to use cannabis despite having physical or psychological problems with it?

If you answered 'yes' to three or more of these seven questions you're likely to be addicted to the substance or behaviour.

Appendix 3

Dreams, dawns, dying:
Self-guided exercises

(Exercises for Chapter 8)

1. Your way to go
Don't read this until you have half an hour of quiet, uninterrupted time to do the exercise. When you are ready, get some paper and a pen, read these instructions and do the exercise straight away.

Imagine that you are given the gift of choosing how you die. Use this gift to explore what your choices are, and why. For example, would you choose to die instantly, as from some heart attacks where you have no idea that you are about to die and it is all over in a moment? Or would you prefer to know that your death is approaching and be conscious through the process? Would you like to die alone, with one companion or several? Who would you want to be with you? If you prefer to die consciously, imagine your last conversation with the people around you. Where would you like to die? What kind of funeral would you like? How would you hope to be remembered and appreciated?

Make a note of your choices. Consider sharing them with people close to you.

2. Looking back from beyond
Do not read this exercise until you are ready to do it. Give yourself up to an hour of quiet time, in a place where you can lie down comfortably and where you will not be interrupted. Try to let go of any worries and distractions before you do this exercise. Imagine leaving them all behind you as you step over a threshold into a special space to do this exercise.

This process invites you to imagine your death and what may lie beyond it, so that you in the present can receive advice from this future point. Read these instructions in full a couple of times, then lie down, close your eyes and relax into the journey.

Imagine that you are in the last minutes of your life. Feel your breath becoming longer, slower, weaker. Sense the life energy flowing out of your body as you become very still. Imagine the moment of your death: see how it feels and notice your emotions. Lie still, silent and receptive, imagining as fully as possible that you are now dead. Don't try to force ideas or make something happen: just be receptive to whatever sense comes to you of any life and awareness beyond physical dying. If such a sense comes to you, ask it to look back at the living you at the present time and ask what advice it may have for you. Thank it for any insights you receive and very slowly bring your awareness back into your living body in the present time. Slowly reflect on the whole experience, allow any feelings to come up and wait until you feel ready before you move back into everyday life.

Index